THE CIRCLE OF THE SUN

Books by Traleg Kyabgon

How To Do Life: A Buddhist Perspective, Shogam Publications, 2021, 9780648686347.

Actuality Of Being: Dzogchen and Tantric Perspectives, Shogam Publications, 2020, 9780648332176.

Vajrayana: An Essential Guide to Practice, Shogam Publications, 2020, 9780648332152.

Desire: Why It Matters, Shogam Publications, 2019, 9780648129318.

Luminous Bliss: Self-realization Through Meditation, Shogam Publications, 2019, 9780980502251.

Integral Buddhism: Developing All Aspects of One's Personhood, Shogam Publications, 2018, 9780648114802.

King Doha: Saraha's Advice to a King, Shogam Publications, 2018, 9780648114864.

Song of Karmapa: The Aspiration of the Mahamudra of True Meaning by Lord Rangjung Dorje, Shogam Publications, 2018, 9780648114864.

Karma: What it is, What it isn't, and Why it matters, Shambhala Publications, 2015.

Four Dharmas of Gampopa, KTD Publications, 2013.

Asanga's Abhidharmasamuccaya, KTD Publications, 2013.

The Essence of Buddhism: An Introduction to Its Philosophy and Practice, Shambhala Publications, 2002 & 2014, 9781590307885.

Ninth Karmapa Wangchuk Dorje's Ocean Of Certainty, KTD Publications, 2011.

Influence of Yogacara on Mahamudra, KTD Publications, 2010.

The Practice of Lojong: Cultivating Compassion through Training the Mind, Shambhala Publications, 2007.

Mind at Ease: Self-Liberation through Mahamudra Meditation, Shambhala Publications, 2004.

Photo facing page: Traleg Kyabgon Rinpoche the Ninth

THE CIRCLE OF THE SUN

Traleg Kyabgon

Foreword by Orgyen Chowang Rinpoche

SHOGAM
PUBLICATIONS
2022

Shogam Publications Pty Ltd
PO Box 239 Ballarat Central
Victoria, Australia, 3353
www.shogam.org
info@shogam.com

Edited by Susan Howes and David Bennett
Designed by David Bennett

Library Reference
Kyabgon, Traleg, 1955
The Circle of the Sun: Heart Essence of Dzogchen

Printed book ISBN: 978-0-6486863-8-5 (Paperback)
E-book ISBN: 978-0-6486863-9-2

DEDICATION

May all sentient beings become
illuminated by the light rays of rigpa.

Contents

Foreword

It is my great pleasure and honor to introduce Traleg Kyabgon Rinpoche's translation and commentary on Tsel Natsok Rangdrol's *The Circle of the Sun*. Tsel Natsok Rangdrol's text has been highly recommended for reading, study and contemplation by great luminaries of the Vajrayana tradition such as H. H. Dilgo Khyentse Rinpoche and Tulku Urgyen Rinpoche. Moreover, Traleg Rinpoche brings his uniquely modern perspective to the elucidation of the text. Not only does he provide the erudition of a great pandita to his explanations, but, perhaps even more importantly for contemporary readers, he speaks from his personal experience, which gives his work the nectar-like flavor of the most profound pith instructions in language especially suited to today's students and practitioners. So right here, we have the great depth of scholarly description and thorough logical analysis from a master of Dzogchen and Mahamudra, as well as the great courage and fearless personal approach to practice that Traleg Rinpoche brought to all of his teachings. I hope many people take this opportunity to drink deeply from the overflowing cup of Traleg Rinpoche's wisdom.

Orgyen Chowang Rinpoche
San Francisco Bay Area 2022

Biography of the Author
TRALEG KYABGON RINPOCHE IX

Traleg Kyabgon Rinpoche IX (1955-2012) was born in Nangchen in Kham, eastern Tibet. He was recognized by His Holiness XVI Gyalwang Karmapa as the ninth Traleg tulku and enthroned at the age of two as the supreme abbot of Thrangu Monastery. Rinpoche was taken to Rumtek Monastery in Sikkim at the age of four where he was educated with other young tulkus in exile by His Holiness Karmapa for the next five years.

Rinpoche began his studies under the auspices of His Eminence Kyabje Thuksey Rinpoche at Sangngak Choling in Darjeeling. He also studied with a number of other eminent Tibetan teachers during that time and mastered the many Tibetan teachings with the Kagyu and Nyingma traditions in particular, including the *Havajra Tantra*, *Guhyasamaja Tantra*, and the third Karmapa's *Zabmo Nangdon* (*The Profound Inner Meaning*) under Khenpo Noryang (abbot of Sangngak Choling). Rinpoche studied the *Abhidharmakosha*, *Pramanavarttika*, *Bodhisattvacharyavatara*, *Abhidharmasamuccaya*, *Six Treaties of Nagarjuna*, the *Madhyanta-vibhaga*, and the *Mahayanuttaratantra* with Khenpo Sogyal. He also studied with Khenpo Sodar and was trained in tantric ritual practices by Lama Ganga, who had been specifically sent by His Holiness Karmapa for that purpose.

In 1967 Rinpoche moved to the Institute of Higher Tibetan Studies in Sarnath, and studied extensively for the next five years. He studied Buddhist history, Sanskrit, and Hindi, as well as Longchenpa's *Finding Comfort and Ease* (*Ngalso Korsum*), *Seven Treasuries* (*Longchen Dzod Dun*), *Three Cycles of Liberation* (*Rangdrol Korsum*), and *Longchen Nyingthig* with Khenchen Palden Sherab Rinpoche and Khenpo Tsondru.

When Rinpoche had completed these studies at the age of sixteen, he was sent by His Holiness Karmapa to study under the auspices of the Venerable Khenpo Yesha Chodar at Sanskrit University in Varanasi for three years. Rinpoche was also tutored by khenpos and geshes from all four traditions of Tibetan Buddhism during this time.

Rinpoche was subsequently put in charge of Zangdog Palri Monastery (the glorious copper colored mountain) in Eastern Bhutan and placed under the private tutelage of Dregung Khenpo Ngedon by His Holiness Karmapa to continue his studies of Sutra and Tantra. He ran this monastery for the next three years and began learning English during this time.

From 1977 to 1980, Rinpoche returned to Rumtek in Sikkim to fill the honored position of His Holiness' translator, where he dealt with many English-speaking Western visitors.

Rinpoche moved to Melbourne, Australia in 1980 and commenced studies in comparative religion and philosophy at LaTrobe University. Rinpoche established E-Vam Institute in Melbourne in 1982 and went on to establish further Centers in Australia, America, and New Zealand. For the next 25 years Rinpoche gave weekly teachings, intensive weekend courses, and retreats on classic Kagyu and Nyingma texts. During this time Rinpoche also taught internationally travelling extensively through America, Europe, and South East Asia and was appointed the Spiritual Director of Kamalashila Institute in Germany for five years in the 1980's.

Rinpoche established a retreat center, Maitripa Centre in Healesville, Australia in 1997 where he conducted two public retreats a year. Rinpoche founded E-Vam Buddhist Institute in the U.S in 2000, and Nyima Tashi Buddhist Centre in New Zealand in 2004. In 2010 Rinpoche established a Buddhist college called Shogam Vidhalaya at E-Vam Institute in Australia and instructed students on a weekly basis.

Throughout his life Rinpoche gave extensive teachings on many aspects of Buddhist psychology and philosophy, as well as comparative religion, and Buddhist and Western thought. He was an active writer and has many titles to his name. Titles include: the best selling *Essence of Buddhism; Desire: Why It Matters; Vajrayana: An Essential Guide to Practice; Moonbeams of Mahamudra; Karma What It Is, What It Isn't, and Why It Matters; The Practice of Lojong;* and many more. Many of Rinpoche's books are translated into a number of different languages including Chinese, French, German, Korean, and Spanish. Rinpoche's writings are thought provoking, challenging, profound, and highly relevant to today's world and its many challenges.

Rinpoche was active in publishing during the last two decades of his life, beginning with his quarterly magazine *Ordinary Mind,* which ran from 1997 to 2003. Further, Rinpoche founded his own publishing arm Shogam Publications in 2008 and released a number of books on Buddhist history, philosophy, and psychology and left instructions for the continuation of this vision. His vision for Shogam and list of titles can be found at www.shogam.com.

Rinpoche's ecumenical approach can be seen in his other activities aimed at bringing buddhadharma to the West. He established the biannual Buddhism and Psychotherapy Conference (1994 - 2003), and Tibet Here and Now Conference (2005), and the annual Buddhist Summer School (1984 to the present).

Traleg Kyabgon Rinpoche IX passed into parinirvana on 24 July 2012, on Chokhor Duchen, the auspicious day of the Buddha's first teaching. Rinpoche stayed in meditation (*thugdam*) for weeks after his passing. A traditional cremation ceremony was conducted at Maitripa Centre and a stupa was erected on the center's grounds in Rinpoche's honor.

It is a privilege to continue Rinpoche's vision and initiatives, and to continue to make the profound teachings of Traleg Kyabgon Rinpoche IX given in the West for over 30 years available through his Centers' activities and Shogam Publications. Rinpoche's Sangha hope that many will benefit.

Acknowledgements

Traleg Rinpoche 9th was a true Dzogchen master who brought the profound teaching of *The Circle of the Sun* to his students. This book is an expression of our appreciation for his presence in our lives.

Gratitude is extended to Claire Blaxell for her special gift of proofreading to finesse the transition from the spoken to the written word, reflecting its authentic intention.

Thank you to the transcribers, and to Sal Celiento for his final proofread.

We would like to recognize the role of Traleg Khandro in nurturing Shogam Publications and enabling these unblemished teachings to see the light of day.

Thank you to the reader.

May the enlightened intent of Traleg Rinpoche's translation shine.

Susan Howes & David Bennett

Editors' Introduction

Dzogchen is the pinnacle of the nine *yanas*[1] of the *Nyingma*[2] tradition of Tibetan Buddhism. Within the vast collection of Dzogchen teachings, *trekcho* and *thogal*, the two main topics of *The Circle of the Sun*, are regarded as the most essential and expedient methods for realization and full attainment of buddhahood. Trekcho means "cutting through," and reveals the view of primordial purity beyond conceptual elaboration through combining intrinsic awareness and emptiness. Thogal means "leaping over," and is related to the integration of appearance and emptiness, working with the inherent luminosity[3] and bringing about realization of spontaneous presence.

The Circle of the Sun was written by Tsele Natsok Rangdrol, who was born in 1608 near the border of the Tibetan provinces of Kongpo and Dakpo. He was recognized as the immediate incarnation of Tenzin Dorje[4] and also as an incarnation of Gotsangpa,[5] a great master of the *Drukpa Kagyu*[6] lineage, an emanation of Milarepa.[7] In his youth he studied with Tsuglag Gyatso, the Third Pawo Rinpoche,[8] and the famous terton, Jatson Nyingpo,[9] as well as other great teachers of the Kagyu[10] and Nyingma lineages. Jamyang Khyentse Chokyi Lodro[11] and Dilgo Khyentse Rinpoche[12] encouraged the study of his writings, as they are particularly suited to beings of these times.[13] Traleg Kyabgon Rinpoche translated The Circle of the Sun while conducting classes for his *ngondro*[14] students. His translation is clear and easily understood.

The text is presented in three sections. The first is The Ground, the starting point which distinguishes the ground of primordially free nature, our authentic state which is complete in itself, from the ground of confusion, the basis for *samsaric*[15] experience.

The second is The Path, consisting of the practices of trekcho and thogal. The trekcho segment points out the difference between the empirical mind and primordial awareness, discusses *shamatha* and *vipashyana* meditation, non-duality, the stages of meditative experience, the comparison between *Mahamudra*[16] and Dzogchen, the three aspects of wisdom, and how to continue in the practice.

The thogal aspect is presented in two stages—how the state of one's authentic being exists in itself, and how that authentic state becomes realized. It covers the energy pathways, the lamps, essential points of practice, the manifestation of the four visions of thogal, and concludes with enhancement, how a practitioner conducts themselves.

The final section is Fruition, the exhaustion of all defilements and full realization of one's authentic condition, manifesting as the three aspects, or *kayas*, of buddha's being.

Traleg Rinpoche concludes his translation with a concise summary of *The Circle of the Sun*, recommending students study and review it repeatedly, and states, "As I went through the text, I found it so inspiring and profound—it is the best summary of Dzogchen teachings I have ever seen."

Although *The Circle of the Sun* is a comprehensive text on trekcho and thogal, it must be emphasized that it should not be regarded as a practice manual for thogal. In order to engage in the practice of thogal one must be stabilized in trekcho and have been given transmission and instruction by an authentic master.

Susan Howes & David Bennett

THE CIRCLE OF THE SUN

PROLOGUE

Among the various and diverse teachings propounded by the buddhas and bodhisattvas with their skilful means, the teachings on Dzogchen should be placed at the apex of the Buddhist tradition. Dzogchen is comparable to the brass top of a victory banner. The four divisions or cycles of Dzogchen consist of the outer Mind Cycle, (Tib. *chi kor*), considered to be external teachings; the inner Space Cycle, (Tib. *nang kor*), which relates to the inner teachings; the Secret Cycle, (Tib. *sang kor*), known as "the Cycle of Pith Instructions"; and the final division which relates to the teachings belonging to the category of the secret-most pith instructions, known as "the Cycle of Supreme-Most Instructions," (Tib. *yang sang lana mepe kor*). This text will present the essential meaning of the *nyingtik* teachings, the *Heart Essence Teachings*, drawn from these four divisions of Dzogchen tantras.[17]

This endeavor to present the Dzogchen teachings in a very simple and straightforward manner will be conducted by setting forth the text in three stages. The first section of the text explains the ground by relating the ground of being to the experiences of samsara and nirvana, or bondage and liberation. The second section explains the path, and according to the Dzogchen teachings, the path is traversed by practicing two methods of Dzogchen known as trekcho and thogal; trekcho means "cutting through," and thogal means "leaping over." Finally, the conclusion of the text will contain descriptions of the fruition stage in relation to the physical and mental attributes of the enlightened being.

SECTION ONE

The Ground

The ground of being can be viewed from two different perspectives. The first is an intellectual understanding, which is inadequate, and the second perspective concerns the ground of being in its actuality. Intellectually, the ground of being has been described in various ways but the following six are quite common descriptions:

> Sometimes the ground of being is referred to as "spontaneously established."
> Some describe the ground of being as "non-determinate."
> Sometimes the ground of being is said to have determinate characteristics.
> The ground of being is sometimes presented as "mutable."
> The ground of being is also said to be apprehensible in varieties of ways.
> And lastly, it is said that the ground of being manifests in diverse forms.

From the perspective of Dzogchen, attempting to understand the ground of being from any of these six perspectives is inadequate; they are only partial and incomplete. To try to intellectually understand the ground of being as "spontaneously established" is a perspective that is not free from difficulties. If the ground of being is understood as being spontaneously established, then the virtues and vices associated with the experiences of samsara and nirvana would also have to be spontaneously established within that state of being, which contradicts the concept of the ground of being as primordially pure. It would then become very difficult to embark on the path and engage in practices such as cutting through and leaping over. Were a practitioner to embark on such a path, if the virtues and vices are spontaneously established within the ground of being, then it would be difficult to understand how liberation may be secured.

If the ground of being is understood as indeterminate, then the thought formulations or conceptual categories imposed on the ground of being should present no problem. Yet if the ground of being is understood as being indeterminate, then even when liberation has been achieved there is no certainty that a relapse may not occur.

On the other hand, the perspective of seeing the ground of being as determinate presents problems of equal gravity. Since the ground of being is seen as having certain determinate characteristics and attributes that are perceived to be immutable and not subject to malleability, it is difficult to understand how the practitioner would then have any success with the reduction of the numerous defilements and obscurations.

If the ground of being is understood as mutable, subject to change, then even if one has been able to attain the fruition stage, it would be possible to forfeit that.

In the event that the ground of being is understood as something open and amenable to conceptual categories, then this could lead to different distorted views such as eternalism[18] or nihilism.[19]

Finally, for the perspective that holds that the ground of being itself can manifest in various forms on the empirical level, this also presents problems, because whatever manifests as being this or that cannot be the ground of being, which is primordially pure.

Whatever perspective one may have on the ground of being

cannot be complete or adequate, precisely because it is intellectual. Because they are perspectives by nature, they do not have an all-encompassing view or understanding—they can only be partial and incomplete.

For this reason, the tantra, *Dra Thalgyur*, says:

> Various perspectives on the ground of being have been put forward—it is spontaneously established, it is mutable, it is indeterminate, it is unchanging, it is determinate, it can manifest in varieties of forms, it is amenable to conceptual thought-forms, and it is primordially pure. It is possible to adopt many different perspectives, such as these. However, they can never provide an all-encompassing view of the ground of being because it is something that cannot be understood in its completeness from any perspective.

In a similar vein, the tantra, *The Mirror of the Mind of Samantabhadra*,[20] has said:

> These perspectives are the creation of various thought-forms, but the ground of being is pure in its own nature.

All these perspectives on the ground of being should be seen as just perspectives. They are intellectual ways of viewing the ground of being and cannot provide a direct experience of it.

The Ground of Primordially Pure Nature

In this context the ground of being should be understood as having none of the characteristics of "thinghood," which avoids the extreme of eternalism. However, the ground of being has various qualities in abundance, which are spontaneously present. Thus it does not fall into the extreme of nihilism, the category of nonexistence. What is referred to as "the ground of being," consists of the coexistence of emptiness, which is the sphere of reality, and authentic wisdom. These two aspects of the ultimate reality coexist in such a manner that they do not come together as two entities, and they are not separable. What the ground of being is in actuality cannot be fully articulated through the use of words and language, since it is not different from *dharmakaya* or the authentic aspect of buddha's being.

So the ground of being is perceived as being primordially pure, free from corruption and embellishment. The ground of being, which is referred to as the "basis," has three aspects: essence, nature, and responsiveness.

The essence of the ground of being is related to the concept of primordial purity.

The nature, in this context, signifies the aspect of spontaneous presence.

The union of these two, nature and essence, produces what is known as "pure creativity," which is referred to as "responsiveness," and is seen as the creative expression of the ground of being assuming various forms of expression in the world.

These three aspects of the ground of being or *gzhi* are no different in terms of their nature, but conceptually, for purposes of explanation, the ground of being can be understood as having these three aspects.

The text, *Heart Mirror of Vajrasattva,*[21] states:

> The ground of being should be understood from the perspectives of essence, nature, and responsiveness.

In a similar vein, the tantric text, *Jewel Garland*, makes the following point:

> The essence of the ground of being is primordial purity, *kadag*, and it transcends the domain of verbal discourse. The nature signifies spontaneous presence, which indicates a sense of completeness and fulfillment. Responsiveness signifies natural expression or self-manifestation.

From the point of view of essence, in relation to the ground of being, various synonyms can be used, such as kadag or primordial purity, *gnas lugs* or the natural state, *ying* or primordial space, the absolute truth, self-existing awareness, emptiness of dharmakaya, and luminosity of *dharmadhatu*. The aspect of the essence of the ground of being has many names, but it is essential to understand that, in spite of that, in itself, it is free from all manner of conceptual categories such as happiness or unhappiness, existence or nonexistence, being this rather than that, being eternal or impermanent, liberation or bondage, nescience or omniscience. The essence of the ground of being cannot be encapsulated in these conceptual formulations, so the essence is non-vitiated by these and other similar conceptual categories. However, this essence of the ground of being is the very thing that is present in such sublime beings as Samantabhadra who is the embodiment of dharmakaya, yet it is no different from what is present in mere insects. The essence is all-pervasive and ever-present, so it does not distinguish or discriminate between various forms of existence and the various levels of existence or being.

The *Mahayana Uttaratantra* or *Ratnagotravibhaga* says:

> This state of openness, which is without beginning and end, is the natural state of all existing entities. Because of its presence, sentient beings have the opportunity to attain nirvana.

This natural state of being, which is the essence aspect of the ground of being, has been variously referred to as "primordial purity" and in the Mahamudra teachings as "Mahamudra of the natural state."

Some scholars and meditators belonging to the New School[22] have criticized the position that the Nyingmapas have taken regarding the question of the essence and have advanced objections to the whole concept of primordial purity. These scholars and meditators of the New School should realize that nothing novel or unusual has been introduced with the concept of primordial purity. Misunderstandings may have emerged as a consequence of semantics, rather than from what is meant by this expression. When the word kadag is used, these people of the New School automatically assume that something new has been said, and that it refers to something totally different from what previous traditions have spoken about.

That is not how it is, because similar expressions can be found in other Mahayana[23] texts, where there is the concept of "purity from the beginning," or "intrinsic purity." The idea of kadag, primordial purity, is something very similar to that, so if the concept of kadag is found to be objectionable, then associated ideas already present in Mahayana teachings must also be objectionable. Not only would the Mahayana concept of buddha-nature come under attack, but the Mahamudra teachings of the New School would come under fire as well since Mahamudra teachings make constant reference to the natural state, which is not different from the Dzogchen concept of kadag, or primordial purity. It is important to realize that the Dzogchen concept of primordial purity does not distort the Buddhist teachings in any way.

At this point someone may pose the question, "If the essence of the ground of being is emptiness, then does that mean voidness?" The simple answer to that is, "No, it does not." Of course, from the point of view of essence, the ground of being is free from all description, explanation and conceptual formulation and transcends ratiocination altogether. From the point of view of nature, there is the concept of spontaneous presence, the sense of fulfillment and completeness in terms of luminosity. Furthermore, with the aspect of responsiveness, the unceasing manifestation of various thought-forms and experiences appear as creative activities.

The ground of being does not fall into the extremes of existence or nonexistence, because the ground of being embodies the essential qualities of emptiness, luminosity, and self-existing awareness.

The text, *The Tantra of Luminosity and Primordial Space*, states:

> Essence is the wisdom of primordial purity, therefore it is free from nescience and conceptual categories. Nature expresses spontaneous presence, which signifies the non-divisibility of emptiness and luminosity. The third aspect of the ground of being, responsiveness, represents the unceasing experiences that manifest in relation to one's mind and the external world.

To put it briefly, in relation to the three aspects of the ground of being, the essence refers to "the non-divisibility of emptiness and self-existing awareness." Nature means "the non-divisibility of emptiness and luminosity." Responsiveness is "the non-divisibility of emptiness and phenomenal experiences," the experiences of the phenomena.

The Ground of Confusion

Having explained that the primordial ground has three aspects, that its essence is primordial purity, its nature is spontaneous presence or clarity, and its aspect of responsiveness arises as unceasing phenomenal experiences, then the question of how confusion has arisen in respect to the concept of primordial purity needs to be addressed. One may wonder how there can be any confusion if the essence of the ground of being is primordially pure.

The origin of confusion and the samsaric experience consequent to that, have to be understood in relation to the other two aspects of the ground of being, namely its nature and responsiveness. From the point of view of essence, nothing could give rise to confusion, because the essence of the ground of being is unconditioned. So the origin of samsara lies in the expression of the other two aspects of the ground of being.

The tantric text, *Auspicious Beauty*, says:

> There is not even a residue of confusion in the essence of
> the ground of being, but the delusions of the mind arise
> from creative activities, which are the spontaneous
> expression of the aspects of nature and responsiveness.

In terms of its essence, the ground of being is completely
unconditioned and is therefore unchanging and permanent, so the
question of confusion does not arise. From the depth of that
unconditioned reality arises the unceasing self-display of the mind.
The nature then manifests as spontaneous presence and
responsiveness and gives rise to the possibility of confusion.

The example of space is used to describe how this process occurs.
Space is completely unconditioned, a state of total openness, yet
clouds are formed in space due to the coming together of causes
and conditions. In a similar way, there is no confusion to be found
in the essence of the ground of being, but due to the self-display of
the other two aspects of the ground of being, namely its nature and
responsiveness, then confusion comes into existence. In Dzogchen
teachings it is said that primordial purity is comparable to a lamp
enclosed in a vase or statue. When the vase is broken, then the
capacity of the lamp to illuminate becomes actualized.

When wisdom is cultivated along the path, the intrinsic
awareness is activated and comes to the fore, rather than remaining
hidden or concealed. Once the primordial awareness or intrinsic
awareness known as *rigpa* is activated, it manifests in eight different
ways. The radiancy of the intrinsic awareness begins to shine forth
as five different lights, and this is known as "the self-display of the
ground of being." As for the eight different modes through which
the primordial awareness or intrinsic awareness is expressed as
spontaneous presence—first it expresses itself as responsiveness,
then as light, as the authentic aspect of the physical body, as
wisdom, and as non-dual experience. It also manifests as freedom,

in terms of being free from extremes, and it can be expressed too in the deluded form of the samsaric experience. Lastly, it can express itself through the experience of enlightenment.

Although eight modes of expression are usually described in the text, nonetheless they can be reduced to the latter two, namely the pure and impure experiences of sentient beings. These different expressions of the intrinsic awareness can be related to spontaneous presence. For example, when the mind has become purified of defilements, then the authentic aspects of the body and mind become actualized and reveal themselves as the purified form of body and immaculate wisdom. Other dimensions include the dimensions of the expression of *sambhogakaya*, which is the authentic form of communication, and that of *nirmanakaya*, which is the authentic form of qualities. All of these refer to the non-diluted, non-deluded expressions of the mind. Another dimension of the experience is responsiveness, which gives rise to the samsaric or impure experiences, and these reveal themselves as dreamlike.

It should be realized that all the different dimensions of experience, and the varied expressions of primordial awareness or intrinsic awareness, have their origins in the ground of being. Nothing can be experienced outside it. All these dimensions of experience, in both their pure and impure forms, have to be seen as the self-display of the ground of being. In the first moment of practice, the meditator has to realize, to determine, that all these manifestations of the mind, the various expressions of the mind— in the broader sense of mind which covers all the different expressions of the ground of being—are simply that, expressions, and they do not have their origin elsewhere.

In the second moment, when the wisdom free from delusion has risen due to practice and becomes fully matured, then the ground of being itself will be understood as the fruition. To attain enlightenment is not to acquire a new state of being or a new form of existence. A revelation dawns on the meditator when they realize that the fruition is no different from the ground of being itself, which has been present from the beginning. This form of insight that a meditator develops is known as "self-liberation." In the Dzogchen teachings, this state is referred to as "Samantabhadra," the symbol for the original state of being, which is not conditioned by the experiences of samsara or nirvana.

When the meditator is not distracted by the self-display of the spontaneous presence, but is able to recognize that all these various expressions are expressions of the ground of being, of the aspect of essence, then everything becomes self-liberated.

With this recognition, the practitioner of Dzogchen realizes Samantabhadra, which is the symbolic representation of one's original nature. Confusion arises when one does not recognize the expressions of the essence for what they are, failing to see them as spontaneous presence. When this occurs, the origin of confusion becomes established. That is the basis from which the confusion of sentient beings of the three realms has arisen.

In the common teachings of Mahayana Buddhism, this is sometimes referred to as the *alaya*, or ground of existence. The alaya can be understood in different ways—for example, if a person is able to engage in a form of spiritual practice, then it serves as the basis to achieve liberation. At the same time, if no practice has been undertaken and the person remains an ordinary sentient being, then the alaya serves as the precondition for the perpetuation of samsaric existence. In this case the alaya becomes the receptacle of the karmic impressions and tendencies. In the common teachings of the Mahayana, there are statements to be found which say that the alaya is the basis of everything, because even nirvana is dependent upon it.

The *Thalgyur* states:

Not knowing, failure to recognize one's own true nature

is contemporary with the origin of samsaric existence.

At this point, one may wonder: "If the practitioner of Dzogchen realizes that the aspect of essence is pure from the beginning and nature is nothing other than the spontaneous expression of that and everything dissipates into the original purity of the ground of being, is there a possibility that confusion and obscurations of the mind may arise again?" However, there can never be regression once insight has been gained into one's authentic condition, so it is therefore not possible to suffer a reversal process.

Purity is spoken about in two ways:

The first relates to the primordial purity, the aspect of essence of the ground of being, which refers to the natural freedom of one's true condition—primordial freedom.

Secondly, purity can be spoken about in relation to practice. Through practice, one comes to have an understanding of that primordial purity and realizes what can be described as "consequential freedom," the freedom that results from having insight into the primordial purity, which is naturally free.

In trying to understand these different types of freedom and purity, we come to understand that there is no cause. There are no causes and conditions to bring about regression in terms of a loss of insight into the original understanding of the ground of being. To clarify this point, the example can be used of an individual who has been afflicted with the plague. With medication, that person's health becomes restored. All the causes and conditions that were present for the persistence of the disease have been obliterated, and the person has been cured.

The example of a seedling can also be used. If the seedling has been burnt or destroyed, it has no potency to give rise to the growth of a certain type of plant, such as a fruit tree. Once insight into the ground of being has been attained, there is no need for anxiety that this insight may be lost due to causes or conditions, because those very causes and conditions have been eliminated.

The words "ordinary sentient beings" relate specifically to the situation where these beings have not had insight into the original purity of the ground of being. It is due to this failure that ordinary sentient beings see things dualistically. The spontaneous presence, the expressions of the nature that have manifested from the aspect of the essence of the ground of being—is seen as being different from the ground of being itself. The spontaneous display of the ground of being is seen as existing independently from the aspect of the essence of the ground of being.

The origin of the confusion lies in this fundamental misapprehension of the relationship between the essence and nature of the ground of being.

The text, *Luminosity of the Lamp*, has this to say:

> From the existential condition of the ground of being, arise the causes and conditions of ignorance or confusion. When the radiance of the mind is not apprehended properly, the dualistic notion of subject and object develops, because a rupture has been introduced between the ground of being and its manifestation as spontaneous presence. In this way, three different types of ignorance come into being.

Firstly, there is the ignorance of not recognizing the ground of being for what it is.

The second type is the co-emergent ignorance, which means that ignorance has been there right from the beginning.

The third type is the ignorance of fixation. When the spontaneous presence or the various expressions of the nature of the ground of being are misconstrued as being real, existing things and entities in the world, then one becomes fixated on the notion of subject and object.

These three types of ignorance should be seen as different

expressions of the same ignorance rather than as existing separately, independent of each other. These three expressions of ignorance are the actual causes for the continuation of samsaric existence.

There are three conditions requiring discussion in regard to how confusion comes into being, and why it persists.

The first is known as "causal condition," and this refers to the condition of not recognizing the three aspects of the ground of being and their interrelationship, namely essence, nature, and responsiveness.

The second is called "object condition," which refers to the expression of the nature in terms of manifesting as inseparable luminosity and emptiness—and thus, everything is expressed as spontaneous presence.

The third condition is "condition of fixation." When ordinary beings do not understand the nature of spontaneous presence as indivisible luminosity and emptiness, then the dualistic concept of subject and object arrives on the scene.

The ignorance and confusion have been brought into being and are perpetuated due to the coming together of the three causes and three conditions.

Confusion and ignorance have resulted from not understanding the workings of the aspects of nature and responsiveness, not in relation to the essence, because the essence is emptiness and is therefore primordially pure. After attaining enlightenment, the activities of nature and responsiveness continue, but while remaining in the samsaric condition, one experiences those differently. The ego's basis relates to nature and responsiveness, as ego is something that one has created.

From the Dzogchen point of view, that does not mean that one's relative concept of ego is something to get rid of. The practitioner needs to understand it for what it is. The ego exists only on the relative level and does not have real inherent existence. After becoming enlightened, the aspect of the relative existence of ego is still there, not changed.

According to Buddhism, generally, and the Dzogchen teachings, the ego is not a unitary, irreducible entity, but is complex. Memory and history and the like are what constitute the ego, and that will continue as long as one lives. An individual was born in a particular place, went to a school, was born into a family, has a name, an occupation—all of these things are relevant to the concept of who one is. Buddhism says that is all there is to the concept of ego or self and thinking that there is more to it than that is mistaken. That is why in Buddhism, the ego is called an aggregate; they have the same meaning. Failing to think of it as an aggregate is what causes confusion regarding one's concept of the ego or self.

Again, overcoming ego does not mean getting rid of it, because that cannot be done practically, even if one wanted to. If a person was born Caucasian and is a particular age, then those things have relevance and one cannot deny or change that. In terms of one's past history and memories, all of those things are relevant. Their coming together constitutes what one is and what one is is not one single factor. It is a group, a corporate entity; one needs to have that concept of the self or ego. That is why it is said that we can change ourselves, meaning that we can introduce various elements into the structure of the ego so that the ego becomes transformed, the self becomes transformed.

When Buddhism speaks about overcoming ego, one should not think that it is about trying to break down one's concept of oneself, knocking the "self" again and again, so that eventually one is left with nothing. That is not the idea at all. To overcome ego does not mean that the self is not important. It means that one has to revise one's concept of the self; one has to have a better understanding of it.

In Dzogchen particularly, an understanding is needed of the

relationship between one's ordinary concept of the self and the ground of being. It is more important to have a better understanding of the ground of being, than to become completely fixated on the concept of the self or ego, and so one has to understand how those two interrelate. The ego, from this point of view, is constructed out of the ground of being. Mistaking the luminous aspect of the ground of being and not recognizing that, gives rise to fixation on the ego. If one recognizes it for what it is, one will not have that fixation. That understanding of the three aspects of the ground of being does not lead to abandonment of the empirical, relative existence of the ego.

The Dzogchen teachings would say that one becomes more of a person through realizing this, than when one remains in that dualistic condition. According to the Dzogchen teachings, this opens one up to the world and to other people, including oneself. Overcoming this dualistic concept does not mean that somehow or other one becomes merged with the greater whole, and ceases to be what one is. That is not what it is about. Individuality is still there, but one is no longer thinking in terms of oneself as a self-existing entity with a substantial reality that exists independent of one's experiences, and of everything else. As was stated previously, the ground of being has three aspects, nature, essence, and responsiveness. In relation to nature and responsiveness, one acts, reacts and interacts, as an individual. In relation to the aspect of essence, one goes beyond one's individuality, because the nature is emptiness.

SECTION TWO

The Path

The ground has been explained in some detail in relation to the experience of liberation or nirvana, and that of bondage or samsara. In order to realize the ground, one has to embark on the path. As mentioned previously, according to the Dzogchen teachings, the path consists of two types of practice: trekcho, which means "cutting through," and thogal, meaning "leaping over." These two practices will be presented separately.

Trekcho—Cutting Through

The Difference between Empirical Mind and Primordial Awareness

First, the practice of trekcho will be presented by distinguishing between the empirical mind or consciousness, *sems*, and primordial awareness, rigpa.

Within the general context of the Mahayana teachings there is consensus regarding the existence of buddha-nature as the capacity for enlightenment within all sentient beings. When engaging in the practice of meditation or any other form of practice, as the delusions peel away, the buddha-nature makes its presence felt. This leads to realization of the authentic physical and mental aspects of buddha's being as the fruition stage of the practice. In this regard there is agreement among all the various teachings of the Mahayana tradition.

However, Dzogchen and Mahamudra understanding differs from the Mahayana concept of buddha-nature in that in Mahayana teachings buddha-nature is potential rather than actual; it has to develop into something else. That is why it is called "the womb of enlightenment," (Skt. *tathagatagarbha*). According to the Mahayana teachings on tathagatagarbha, one has to go through the different paths and stages in order to attain enlightenment. While everyone does have buddha-nature, it is only through practice that it is developed.

Dzogchen and Mahamudra teachings do not see it that way, which is why the Dzogchen and Mahamudra approach is called "the sudden path," and the Mahayana approach is called "the gradual path." The Dzogchenpas say that the ground of being is already complete. Nothing needs to be added or improved upon and nothing new has been uncovered through practice. It is just that the obscurations are peeled away and then the practitioner realizes what is there. In Dzogchen this is referred to as "the ground of being," and in Mahamudra as "the nature of the mind," which is also seen as being already mature and complete.

In this context, according to the practice of trekcho, it is essential to understand the difference between sems and rigpa, or empirical consciousness and primordial awareness.

The essence of the practice is the cultivation of primordial awareness alone. This is a specifically Dzogchen view on the matter. In relation to the concept of the ground of being, as has already been alluded to, there is a difference between the ground of being and the ground of all. It was explained that the nature of the ground of being is primordially pure, or what is called "kadag." This primordial purity has never been corrupted by the delusions and obscurations of the samsaric condition. It is the source from which the various expressions of wisdom arise, and it also provides the appropriate conditions for all the qualities of nirvana to manifest. Yet it cannot be represented as being this or that, and so therefore it is unconditioned since it is not contingent upon anything else. In relation to the ground of being, it is possible too, to speak about establishment of the proper view, the practice of meditation, and engaging in spontaneous activities. It is also from the ground of being itself that various spiritual powers, fearlessness, and non-diluted experiences have their origin.

That is why Dzogchen and Mahamudra teachings use the example of space. Space does not cause the clouds to come into existence but creates room in the first place for the clouds to be there. In a similar way, it is the unconditioned aspect of the ground of being that allows the conditioned mind to operate. To attain enlightenment, according to Dzogchen, is not to go beyond the conditioned mind as much as knowing and understanding that the conditioned aspect is a manifestation of the unconditioned.

By contrast, the ground of all is the basis of samsaric experience itself. It is the repository of the karmic traces and dispositions, and it exists as primordial ignorance, providing the precondition for the emergence of obscurations and delusions of the mind. The ground of all provides the basis upon which the interaction between actions, karmic traces and dispositions, conceptual thought formations, and emotional conflicts occurs. Due to the basis of all, one has the experience of the trinity of the body, phenomena, and the mind. All the experiences related to conditioned phenomena are dependent on the basis of all (Tib. *kun gzhi rnam shes*; Skt. *alayavijnana*). Unlike the ground of being, the basis of all is defective and is something that has to be transcended.

According to Dzogchen teachings, the basis of all can be understood in four different ways, corresponding to its aspects or functions. The first is the aspect of primordial ignorance or co-emergent ignorance. The second relates to the aspect of a repository or container of the karmic traces and dispositions. The third aspect of the ground of all relates to karmic actions, which are responsible for the various experiences associated with samsara and nirvana. The fourth aspect relates to the body, the physical basis of sentient beings dwelling in the three realms of existence: the realm of sensuality or *kamadhatu*, the realm of form or *rupadhatu*, and the realm of formlessness or *arupadhatu*.[24]

The ground of being itself is non-divisible, and it can be understood differently only in terms of its functions. The ground of all is the basis of purification. By contrast, the ground of being is the basis of liberation, the place within which ultimate liberation is attained, and it is primordial purity.

The basis of liberation is not the ground of all, as some people mistakenly assume. The Dzogchen tantra, *Mirror of the Heart*, cautions:

> Those who mistakenly grasp the ground of all as being identical with dharmakaya or the authentic aspect of buddha's being, are deluding themselves.

As for the ground of being, the text, *Garland of Pearls*, states:

> Dharmakaya is devoid of any form of corruption. It embodies the two qualities of emptiness and luminosity, and this natural condition is not subject to the influences of mental activities. It is unconditioned and all-pervasive, just like the space itself, therefore it cannot be represented as being this or that.

Another Dzogchen text, *Self-Awareness of Rigpa*, says:

> The ground of all is the source of all the conceptual thought formations, therefore the ground of all is polluted by all manner of conceptual confusion. So the ground of all is inseparable from ignorance.

These texts emphasize the need to be very clear in terms of distinguishing the primordial purity of the ground of being, which is free from delusions—from the ground of all, which is seen as being the seat of delusions and mental confusion. It could also be of some relevance to recall the discussion on the difference between the aspects of primordial purity and spontaneous presence in this context.

The Difference between Sems and Rigpa

According to Dzogchen teachings, a distinction has to be made between sems and rigpa. Sems refers to the ordinary mind that thinks, remembers, anticipates, feels anxiety, and so on. Rigpa, on the other hand, refers to the primordial awareness, which is present atemporally. In other words, rigpa or primordial awareness is not found in the past, present, or future in a fragmented manner, but is ever-present. The aim of the practice of Dzogchen is orientated toward discovering that primordial awareness, and this is what distinguishes Dzogchen practice from all other practices associated with Buddhism.

The primordial awareness spoken of in Dzogchen teachings is synonymous with the concept of original purity or kadag. The primordial purity is different from the alayavijnana or what is known as the "storehouse consciousness," because the storehouse consciousness is the reservoir of all one's mental experiences in terms of thinking and emotions. The primordial awareness, which is identified with original purity, is the same as dharmakaya, the authentic aspect of buddha's being. One's mental continuum may be tarnished by varieties of experiences originating from the storehouse consciousness; nonetheless the primordial awareness that has been present from the beginning has not suffered any form of corruption or vitiation.

From the Dzogchen point of view, this primordial awareness, innate within one's being, is the source of spiritual realization, and is responsible for giving rise to various qualities and manifestations of the enlightened mind. But in itself, the primordial awareness cannot be said to be this or that. Nothing can be predicated on it, yet at the same time because of it, one has the power to overcome delusions and obscurations of the mind and the possibility of obtaining enlightenment. The reason the primordial awareness in itself cannot be predicated as having this or that quality or attribute is precisely because it is not a thing or entity, hence it goes beyond conceptualization. On the other hand, because of it, all the enlightened qualities of an awakened mind emerge.

In the Dzogchen teachings, as in other Buddhist teachings, when speaking about the view, meditation, and action, the practitioner has to realize that primordial awareness is the basis of these three divisions—the view, meditation, and action. Without the presence of primordial awareness then, it would not be possible to speak about view, meditation, or action. When the practitioner of Dzogchen is able to tune into their original awareness, varieties of spiritual powers and fearlessness begin to emerge within their stream of consciousness. The primordial awareness gives rise to the qualities and the attributes of buddhahood, but in itself, the primordial awareness cannot be described as being this, or that.

When we speak about the mind of an ordinary human being, it needs to be understood in relation to the storehouse consciousness, because what is normally regarded as the mind, the one that thinks, anticipates, remembers, feels, and so on, is tied up with one's character, disposition, and propensity. Everything is conditioned; one's thinking and feeling is conditioned both internally and externally. As a result, impressions are left in the mindstream of that individual, the storehouse consciousness.

That is not to say that an individual cannot have certain experiences that are indeterminate, in that when an object is perceived through the sensory organs, one does not judge it to be beautiful, ugly, or repulsive, or that one's feelings are not judged to be pleasurable or painful but interpreted as neutral. By and large, however, everything that is experienced is vitiated or tarnished by one's interpretation of the experience. Because of these interpretations, impressions are left or imprinted on the mindstream of the individual, which constitute the karmic imprints and also their propensities. The imprints of the mind give rise to the karmic propensities, and therefore karmic cause and effect is put into operation through either physical or mental actions.

Physically and in terms of the mind, actions are performed that are either wholesome or beneficial, or unwholesome and harmful.

The repeated exercise of these actions has the potency to create the propensity or disposition to act in a certain way. What is normally called "mind" is not as simple as we assume, because the mind as we understand it has the capacity to radically alter our conception of the body, our perception of the world, and our experience of the inner workings of the mind. According to the Dzogchen teachings, this mind needs to be overcome and transcended if we are to consequently realize the primordial awareness present in each of us.

The distinction made in Dzogchen between sems and rigpa is very unusual because most Buddhist traditions do not make that distinction, speaking instead about sems and *yeshe*; and *namshe*, the deluded mind, and yeshe. Namshe is synonymous with sem, and yeshe is wisdom. In the Lamrim[25] teachings of the graduated path it is said that through the use of sems, gradually, through practice the defilements and delusions are overcome, and then the wisdom mind of the buddha is realized.

In this case it is different. When Lamrim teachings speak about overcoming namshe, the deluded mind, and realizing yeshe or the enlightened mind, they are not referring to overcoming a certain kind of mind and then realizing another kind of mind, but this is exactly what the Dzogchen teachings are saying. Two different natures of the mind are present—one is deluded and the other is not. The non-deluded one is to be realized, and the one that is deluded is to be overcome. The Mahamudra teachings are different again, because we realize that the very mind that we experience is not different from the primordial awareness that the Dzogchenpas speak about.

Divisions of the All-ground

In the Dzogchen teachings, it is absolutely essential to make the distinction between sems and rigpa, between the ordinary empirical consciousness, and primordial awareness. The ordinary consciousness has its basis in the storehouse consciousness, or the all-ground, as discussed. The concept of the storehouse consciousness, the all-ground, can be broken down into several different functions of the mind.

Primordial ignorance, or co-emergent ignorance, relates to the function of the original aspect of the storehouse consciousness. The traces and dispositions of the mind that have accumulated over a long period of time produce tendencies that may lead to the possibility of attaining nirvana, or may inhibit the mind in such a way that samsara continues. This aspect or function of the storehouse consciousness is called "the operational storehouse consciousness." The aspect of physical embodiment, with a variety of creatures of visible shape and form that display characteristics belonging to certain life-forms, is referred to as "the physical expression of the storehouse consciousness."

In this context, there is only one storehouse consciousness or all-ground, but those distinctions can be made in terms of its function. From the point of view of practice, all the functions of the storehouse consciousness have to be brought to an end, because they are vitiated and therefore are to be abandoned. For this reason, the past Dzogchen masters have said that the primordial purity of the mind, kadag, the fundamental ground of being, is the one to work upon and realize, not the all-ground or storehouse consciousness that is part of sems. Kadag, the primordial ground, has been pure right from the beginning. These two grounds have very different characteristics and qualities. The ground of being, which manifests as primordial purity, is the basis of liberation. It is also the goal where all the defilements and obscurations of the mind eventually dissipate and subside, and come to rest naturally. The storehouse consciousness, the all-ground, has to be distinguished from the primordial ground that expresses that fundamental native purity, that intrinsic purity.

The Dzogchen text, *Mirror of the Mind of Samantabhadra*, cautions:

> Those who mistake the all-ground or storehouse consciousness for the dharmakaya, which is the same as kadag, the primordial ground, have gone astray.

The Dzogchen text, *Garland of Pearls*, has stated:

> Dharmakaya by nature is devoid of all defiling tendencies of the mind. It has the characteristic of being empty and luminous, and thoughts and concepts about this and that can have no influence whatsoever on its nature, because it is just like the space, all-pervasive, and therefore it cannot be represented as being this or that.

The Dzogchen tantric text, *Self-Existing Awareness*, says:

> Due to attachment to the storehouse consciousness, variegated forms of conscious thoughts and experiences have risen. Therefore the storehouse consciousness should be viewed as the ground of confusion, rather than the ground of one's being.

The distinction between the all-ground, the storehouse consciousness, and the ground of one's being manifesting as primordial purity has to be made because one is the source of confusion, and the other one is not. When speaking about "the mind," this is the mind that gives rise to varieties of conscious experiences that are momentary, fleeting, and impure. On the other hand, rigpa or primordial awareness has been pure right from the beginning, which is the meaning of kadag. In the sutric teachings, the term "buddha-nature" or tathagatagarbha, refers to the same thing. So, again, the two aspects of the mind are distinctly different in their nature. The ordinary mind that we have access to on a day-to-day level is something that needs to be purified, overcome, and transcended. On the contrary, rigpa or intrinsic awareness is something that needs to be realized. Through realization of primordial awareness or rigpa, one realizes not only the aspect of buddha's being, but also the ultimate reality.

The ordinary mind, which is sems, has the function of generating the samsaric condition, cyclic existence, and reinforcing the dualistic notion of subject and object. From this dualistic notion all the mental afflictions come into being and disturb the mind. The primordial awareness or rigpa is indistinguishable from wisdom and is responsible for realizing all the potentiality of the mind as embodied in the three aspects of buddha's being. So the experience of rigpa or primordial awareness is unitive and not dualistic—it is the experience of *zung 'jug*, which means "unitive." The experience of sems, on the other hand, is divisive and dualistic, arising from the all-ground storehouse consciousness. The ordinary, conscious experiences that an individual has or endures on a day-to-day level are contingent on that, because such experiences leave impressions that are then retained in the storehouse consciousness. This gives rise to the notion of an unchanging, permanent self and other.

These experiences lie at the root of one's delusions. As long as these delusions are operative, then one's own sensory organs and sensory impressions cannot be relied upon, because these further strengthen the delusions already there. The three primary conflicting emotions of attachment, aversion, and ignorance can give rise to five. They multiply, and then we have attachment, aversion, pride, jealousy, and ignorance, and as the mind becomes more and more complex and confused, we have twenty subsidiary emotional conflicts. Tsele Natsok Rangdrol says that it is possible to go on and on, and we can in fact end up with 60 thousand different types of mental conflicts. If we are familiar with psychiatry, this may not be too far off the mark. When the mind is completely dominated by illusion and delusion generated by conflicting emotions and the mistaken belief in the duality of subject and object, we wander in the samsaric condition. No one and nothing else is responsible for this plight other than the mind itself—the sems aspect of the mind.

When looking at rigpa, it is a totally different situation, because primordial awareness by nature is devoid of all affliction—not a trace of delusion or mistaken belief can be found there. The three aspects of buddha's being—dharmakaya, sambhogakaya, and nirmanakaya, are already embodied in that. They are already present waiting to be discovered. As was mentioned earlier when the question of ground was raised, the ground has three aspects, essence, nature, and responsiveness. These three aspects of the ground of being or primordial awareness, in fact correspond to those three aspects of buddha's being, namely dharmakaya, sambhogakaya, and nirmanakaya. Due to the presence of rigpa, instead of falling under the influence of the five poisons or conflicting emotions of attachment, aversion, pride, jealousy, and ignorance, the mind is able to express itself through the avenue of the five wisdoms: mirror-like wisdom, wisdom of equanimity, wisdom of discrimination, wisdom of all-accomplishment, and wisdom of all-encompassing space, or wisdom of ultimate reality.[26] In this way the individual has the capacity to express the further reaches of the mind, because of the activation of wisdom.

All these different functions and kinds of wisdom can be subsumed under two:

One aspect of wisdom relates to seeing things as they are, the wisdom enabling the individual to perceive the ultimate reality as it is, without distortion, and to realize the ultimate truth.

The other aspect relates to understanding varieties of things in the world. This is the wisdom that enables the individual to apprehend and understand empirical phenomena.

Whether enlightenment is able to be achieved does not hinge

on what is done with sems or ordinary consciousness, but rather upon what one is doing with rigpa or primordial awareness. In Dzogchen teachings this distinction is of paramount importance, and has been emphasized over and over in numerous Dzogchen practice manuals.

As the *Garland of Pearls* instructs:

> If one wants to become wise in the practice of *maha ati*[27] or Dzogchen, then that individual must have a proper understanding of the difference between sems and rigpa.

As was noted earlier, it has to be understood that sems is responsible for creating the kind of person one is, because of the interaction between traces and dispositions, the storehouse consciousness, and one's own experiences on a day-to-day level. Through the interaction of these three, all one's experiences in terms of both the physical and mental domains become defiled, since the duality of the perceiver and perceived, or subject and object has not been overcome, and that is the very cause of the samsaric condition. If one is free from the defiling tendencies of sems, then one becomes enlightened and every trace of defilement vanishes. Through a greater understanding of rigpa, one must endeavor to burn the conceptual confusion and delusions, and realize primordial awareness, which simultaneously displays the two qualities of being empty and luminous.

The text, *Six Dimensions of Samantabhadra*, has this to say:

> Oh Mahasattva, those individuals who are unable to differentiate between the nature of sems and rigpa will never come to see the light, just like the sun when it is shrouded in the mist of clouds. If one begins to unlock the secrets of the mind, then that individual will achieve freedom, because they will never be fixated on the concept of the object, that which is to be perceived, or the

perceiver, the subject, since that adherent or yogi has achieved mastery over primordial awareness.

Another example is from the tantric text, *Sutra of Wisdom Gone Beyond*:

> If one realizes the workings of the mind, one becomes a buddha and there is nothing more to it. The buddha and buddhahood cannot be found elsewhere, externally.

When the word "wisdom" is used in this context, it means that wisdom is related to understanding the ordinary mind, sems. If one understands sems and its workings, and does not come under its influence, then one has realized wisdom—if one continues to operate under its influence, then that is ignorance. If the workings of the mind are realized through the use of rigpa, primordial awareness, then the delusions and confusion of the mind generated by the ordinary mind, sems, become dissipated; they vanish automatically.

An example is used to describe how this happens. If a king wanted to invade another country, to conquer that kingdom, instead of killing numerous human beings, all those subjects would automatically come under his power and influence by apprehending or seizing control of the enemy king. In a similar way, instead of dealing with this particular delusion or that specific emotional conflict, by going to the root of it all, the other problems will be solved automatically. In order to practice Dzogchen effectively, it is important to also have familiarity with the conventional tantric practices, and this will be discussed next.

Vajrayana Empowerment

To enter into the practice of the Vajrayana tradition, one has to receive empowerment (Tib. *wang*; Skt. *abhisheka*). The function of empowerment is to mature the student. That needs to be followed by spiritual instructions, and these are orientated toward liberation.

The empowerment matures the student in an appropriate manner, and the instruction liberates that individual, so for a beginner it is important to receive empowerments.

Not all tantric empowerments are the same within Vajrayana Buddhism. Generally speaking, firstly there is the empowerment that emphasizes the outer form as exemplified by the conferring or bestowal of the vase abhisheka, or vase empowerment. The other kinds of empowerment deal with increasingly subtle levels of consciousness, whereby the proliferation of various thoughts and concepts becomes reduced. The secret empowerment is more subtle than the vase empowerment because it does not deal with the external form, but rather with the contents of the mind. That is followed by the wisdom empowerment, which is geared toward producing a state of mind where the mind becomes freed from all its habitual tendencies and preoccupations. This process culminates with the empowerment of what is known as the "word," or "logos," where the true nature of ultimate reality is revealed.

In this context, whether an individual has properly received the appropriate empowerment is not determined simply by their physical attendance, but rather it relates to that individual's mind. If an individual has had the opportunity to attend a tantric empowerment of this nature, that should produce certain inner transformations indicating that the empowerment has had its desired effect. For example, if the student has received the vase empowerment, then they would be able to see and hear things differently. The sensory impressions generally will have become transformed as a consequence of an inner, conscious transformation. The ordinary perceptions of subject and object, the five elements, and the five psychophysical constituents, are seen as expressions of divinity; they become sacred. If an individual was present and had partaken in an initiation or empowerment ceremony, unless this transformation has been experienced, then the individual has not fully received the vase empowerment at all.

Similarly, if a practitioner had been participating in an empowerment ceremony where the secret empowerment was conferred on the participants, then those present should be able to realize all the sounds that one normally encounters on a day-to-day level, as being expressions of the secret mantra. If the individual has failed to do that, it would mean that the secret empowerment has not been received properly.

Furthermore, when the wisdom empowerment that a practitioner has awaited is being imparted, if the individual does not succeed in realizing that everything that occurs in the mind in terms of both positive and negative or wholesome and unwholesome thoughts and emotions are expressions of wisdom itself, but instead continues to entertain the dualistic notion of wisdom and confusion, then the wisdom empowerment has not been fully received.

This series of empowerments is orientated toward producing full recognition of one's true nature, which is dharmakaya. If that has not been realized by the individual, and instead the empowerments are externalized and thought of as being techniques and methods only, rather than the means to provoke or invoke dharmakaya, the true nature of one's being—then the practitioner has failed to receive the word or logos empowerment. At the very best, one should have a thorough understanding of it. If not, one must have some experience in relation to the process that has taken place. At the very least, one must have some intellectual understanding of what is going on.

It is very important to receive these empowerments in full understanding of what is required. Having received the desired empowerment, it is not sufficient to simply think, "I have received it." It is extremely important to dwell upon this point, because in this day and age there are many teachers and students who do not give sufficient thought to what is involved here. They are more concerned with who has received what, and who has imparted which empowerment, and less about whether the empowerment has had any effect, whether it has taken hold of the individuals who have received it. It is extremely important to keep in mind the understanding of *samaya*, the spiritual bond that is established between the teacher and the student. It is essential to examine the characteristics and the qualities of both student and teacher, and the nature of the empowerments: the meaning, the differences between the four empowerments, the type of substances used as part of the ceremonies, and in what manner they are imparted.

The student should try to be informed about these matters before simply plunging into the empowerment. Once the commitment has been made, then the samaya, the spiritual bond, has to be preserved. Many different kinds of samaya bonds are described in the tantric literature, both in the old tantras as well as the new tantras. It is extremely important to realize that an empowerment cannot be taken with a casual attitude; it has to be done properly otherwise there will not be any kind of inner transformation. If it is approached that way, then it will prepare one to proceed along the spiritual path with fewer obstacles and less hardship.

Common and Uncommon Preliminaries

Having established that the empowerment or abhisheka has the function of ripening the spiritual seeds in the practitioner, we now proceed to discussing the process involved with the idea of liberation. At the beginning, before entering into the actual practice of liberation, one must engage in the Common and Uncommon Practices of the Preliminaries.

The Common Preliminary Practices refer to the Four Contemplations—the preciousness of a human birth; impermanence, the conditioned existence; the inviability of the karmic causal nexus; and the suffering of living beings in samsara. The Uncommon Preliminary Practices, or ngondro, involve the Four Foundations—Prostrations, Vajrasattva mantras, Mandala offering, and Guru Yoga. The practitioner must persist with these practices until gaining certain indications of achievement in terms of realization. If the preliminary practices are done prior to engaging in the actual practice of liberation, then the mind would be completely prepared for it. The self-existing awareness would inevitably arise as a consequence of having done these practices.

The Actual Practice of Trekcho

As far as the actual practice is concerned, there are many ways of describing and approaching it, but in this particular context, which is that of Dzogchen, the practice of liberation is approached from the two principal perspectives. As stated previously, one perspective is trekcho, which, again, is generally translated as "cutting through," and the other is thogal, rendered in English as "leaping over." As far as the practice of trekcho or cutting through is concerned, first of all one must establish the proper view regarding the authentic existential condition of the reality. Once able to establish the view, then all manner of doubts and uncertainties will be put aside, and the practitioner will have a real and genuine sense of certainty.

In order to achieve that goal, that certainty, according to Dzogchen practice, first of all the practitioner should examine the unceasing mental activities that go on in the mind. Secondly, the nature of all the mental events needs to be examined. Thirdly, the practitioner has to determine the onset, persistence, and dissipation of those mental activities. The manner in which these three tasks are performed will depend upon the specific, individual instructions provided by the teacher, and also the unique and individual understanding of the student based upon what they have understood intellectually, which leads to inference. The intellectual understanding of the instructions does not give rise to direct experience, but the student is able to form a valid form of inference that is able to guide them to the proper view.

The manner in which interaction between the teacher and student takes place in this process would be intimately connected with the specific situation involved. In order to establish the proper view according to trekcho teachings, the cutting through teachings, first one has to realize that people who are not tutored in religion and philosophy do not have any particular view regarding the authentic existential condition of reality. They are victims of a dualistic way of thinking, which is erroneous—due to that, they suffer from and are afflicted by attraction and aversion. As for some non-Buddhists who are more reflective than the ordinary people, and have contemplated on things that matter and tried to examine and analyze the ultimate reality—usually they have been driven to two extreme types of conclusions. Either they subscribe to a form of eternalist view, or alternatively they come to embrace a form of nihilism. Up to 360 specific instances involving non-Buddhist views have been enumerated, and all of them fall into one or the other of the two categories, namely eternalism or nihilism.

Even among Buddhists, the *shravakas*[28] believe in the reality of the Four Noble Truths: the truth of suffering, the truth of its origination, the truth of its cessation, and the path that leads the individual out of suffering. The *pratyekabuddhas*[29] believe in the reality of the evolution and devolution of the Twelve Interdependent Links.[30] The *bodhisattva*[31] believes in the reality of the two truths, the relative truth and the absolute truth, where the empirical, spatial, temporal world is seen as being the relative truth, and its nature, which is emptiness, is perceived as the ultimate truth. In terms of practice, they also believe in the reality of the two types of *bodhicitta*, with the enlightened compassionate thought in its aspirational form and in its engagement, where they are actually participating in certain activities. Even the bodhisattvas have failed to realize the ultimate truth completely, because there may still be a trace of clinging involved. In terms of their understanding and view, they cling onto the idea of the two truths. In terms of action, there is still an element of attachment remaining because of the bodhisattva concept of the two aspects of bodhicitta, or the enlightened compassionate thought.

The Tantras

Now we come to the Buddhist tantras. The first tantra is the *Kriyatantra*. Its practice involves visualization of manifestations of divinities belonging to the three Buddha families, all of which are peaceful in nature. The manifestation of these divinities is viewed as the relative truth, and the revelation of the ultimate nature of these divinities is understood as being the ultimate or absolute truth. Their nature does not fall into the four extremes of existence or nonexistence, both or neither, both existing and not existing, and neither existing nor non-existing. Those four options are considered to cover all possibilities.

The next two tantras are *Upayatantra* and *Yogatantra*. Both these tantras involve visualization of varieties of deities belonging to five Buddha families, or to hundreds of Buddha families. The phenomenal aspect of these divinities is the relative truth, and that the nature of these divinities is emptiness is accepted as the ultimate truth.

In the following tantra, *Mahayogatantra*, all the sensory impressions, what is perceived visually, audially, nasally, through touch and taste, and all the peaceful and wrathful deities that are visualized through the practice of creative imagination, correspond to the relative truth. These divinities, these deities, do not come into being, do not dwell anywhere, and therefore do not come to cease to exist. In other words, because they do not dwell in the spatial, temporal world, that reveals the ultimate truth. The experience that the practitioner has of the divinities is a unitive experience, because there is no separation between the practitioner who has visualized the deities and the deities themselves.

In the *Anuyogatantra*, the final tantra, the nature of the mind, which has never been tainted or polluted by all that goes on in the mind, by the mental events and processes—is the *ying*, the sphere of the reality. The sphere of reality and the wisdom that enables one to apprehend things immediately and intuitively and not perceive things as objects are understood to be totally inseparable—the sphere of reality and wisdom. Due to that realization, great bliss (Tib. *dewa chenpo*; Skt. *mahasukha*) is attained.

These tantras can be understood in terms of being in groups of five or six, five if one subsumes Upayatantra into Kriyatantra and Yogatantra. The view of Upayatantra is the same as Yogatantra, while the practice is in keeping with the Kriyatantra. If Upayatantra is treated separately, then these tantras could be grouped into six major tantric bodies of teachings. Normally the three outer tantras and three inner tantras are spoken about.

In brief, even with the Buddhist tantras, the realization attained is not complete as there is still an element of clinging and attachment involved. The practitioner is still interested in conditioning the mind through the use of varieties of devices, such as visualization of divinities. In order to go directly to the nature of the mind without resorting to any form of device to bring about realization of the nature of the mind, one needs to engage in the practice of trekcho or cutting through, as described in the Dzogchen teachings.

To understand the Dzogchen view of the authentic existential condition of the reality and to develop a proper view of it, one has to realize that there is no method that can symbolize it, because the nature of the existential condition of the reality is unconditioned wisdom and primordial purity. It cannot be formulated with concepts and ideas, but it exists as the authentic condition of the reality itself. It is the circle of the ultimate reality, the circle which does not have any center or periphery, and it is free from the very beginning, precisely because its nature is emptiness. Therefore it has never come into being.

Because the luminosity aspect of one's authentic condition is unceasing, it serves as the basis for one's experience of samsara and nirvana, and even though one's perceptions and experiences are many and varied, they manifest from this luminous aspect. Nevertheless, none of these can have any effect on the true and authentic condition of the mind itself. Whatever arises in the mind can never deviate from this reality, or ever exist outside of it. This authentic condition is devoid of all empirical characteristics and predication, for it lacks shape, color, and value. The idea of good or evil, even the concepts of existence and nonexistence are not applicable, because it can never be symbolized with any satisfaction.

It should be pointed out that simply thinking that the authentic condition is unoriginated and devoid of all empirical characteristics is not sufficient, because even that is conceptualizing the reality. In order to have the correct view, one even has to learn to let go of the idea that the nature of the mind or the authentic existential condition, is devoid of this and that. Full comprehension of the view is achieved through assimilation of the spiritual instructions received from the teacher, so that doubts and uncertainties and what is called "two-mindedness," are put to rest. Due to that, what is understood is direct and immediate, rather than resulting from mediate and conceptual understanding. This is what is known as having proper understanding of the view.

This immediate understanding means that what is to be understood and the agent who understands are not separate. What is to be understood is seen as having been present within one's own condition, right from the beginning. This does not bring something new into the purview of one's consciousness, but it is a form of recognition, because what needs to be understood has always existed within one's condition. There is no separation between the object that needs to be understood, and the subject who has to understand—that separation, that gap is overcome, therefore it is immediate.

I will now recapitulate some of the points, which may be helpful.

Having established the view in Dzogchen means that one has overcome all manner of doubts and uncertainties, whereby the individual has had a glimpse of the true nature of things, the existential condition of the ultimate reality. From the ultimate point of view, there is no duality between that which has to be known and the knower. That which has to be known, of course, is the ultimate reality, with the knower being the subject, the individual practitioner. The reason this is so is because unlike other forms of knowing available on a day-to-day level, what becomes realized here, what comes to the fore and becomes known is not something new. The object of knowledge in this case has always been part of the subject, the individual knower. Therefore it is referred to as "self-knowledge," which refers to recognizing, re cognizing one's face.

The knowledge attained in terms of the establishment of the view comes about through the retrieval of an insight that has been lost, rather than the practitioner acquiring something completely new. At this point, we are speaking about the Dzogchen view regarding trekcho, cutting through. Questions may be raised regarding the view, because if all it involves is trying to repossess something that is not necessarily lost, but has been put aside, ignored—then is it sufficient to simply recognize that? Is the insight gained simply from knowing that all that is needed is to retrieve that knowledge of the ultimate reality, which has always been part of oneself?

To answer that question it has to be said that it is not sufficient to simply have that understanding. For some exceptional people, that may be adequate, but the majority of sentient beings need to embark on a spiritual path, because they cannot achieve spontaneous realization of this kind. The reason this is so is because one's true existential condition has always been so close to the subject, yet it continues to remain at a distance. That distance or gulf is created by delusions and habitual patterns that are repeated with great persistence, over a long period of time. These well-entrenched habitual patterns need to be deconstructed so that they cease to have an influence on the individual. Where do the habits eventually dissipate? They dissipate into one's own authentic condition.

This particular point can be driven home by finding textual support. Even in the sutric teachings, the non-tantric teachings that do not have a direct relationship with the Dzogchen teachings, this point is reinforced.

From the *Sutra of the Purification of Karma*:

"Oh Tathagata, how is a practitioner able to overcome defilements of the mind? What sort of experiences can one expect from having accumulated various karmic actions in the past? What is the nature of these karmic acts?"

The Buddha, the Tathagata, answered by saying, "The nature of those karmic acts does not deviate from ultimate reality."

The interlocutor persisted, "If that is so, does that mean that all sentient beings would attain buddhahood naturally, because the karmic acts themselves do not deviate from the ultimate reality? Does that mean, whatever one does it does not matter? If whatever action one engages in is performed within the sphere of the ultimate reality, does that mean that one does not need to make any effort to attain buddhahood?"

The Tathagata responded to that question by saying, "That is not so. Just as butter is present in the milk without it being churned, the ultimate reality has always been part of every single, individual sentient being. However, without engaging in the churning process, butter would not be produced. In order to extract butter from milk, one has to churn the milk. Likewise, if a person is looking for silver, that person would not find silver lying around. That person would have to select certain stones knowing that silver is contained in that potential form, and then go through the process of extracting that silver. The relationship between the ultimate reality and ordinary sentient beings is no different from these examples, because even though the ultimate existential condition of each sentient creature is the same, in order to realize that, they have to embark on the spiritual path. If they fail to do that, then the ultimate form of realization, which is buddhahood, is impossible."

The interlocutor went on to say, "If that is so, that the ultimate reality and the authentic existential condition is present in each living being, and at the same time, in order to realize that, one has to engage in a form of practice, how should one think of practice?"

In response the Tathagata said, "One should practice by thinking that the conceptual proliferation and emotional conflicts that afflict the mind and distort one's perception of the true reality should be seen as clouds in the sky," meaning that the confusion and emotional conflicts do not have inherent existence or reality of their own. "Just as even the densest clouds become dispersed, in a similar way all the confusion in the mind is potentially eradicable."

Even after the discussion had gone this far, the enquirer was not satisfied and persisted by saying, "If confusion is accidental, then how can one be sure that once it has disappeared, it will not reappear? It is possible that even when one has attained buddhahood, the confusion may make its reappearance."

The Tathagata made the comment, "That is not possible. When one has attained buddhahood, then one has been able to cut through at the root of conceptual proliferation, just like burning diseased seedlings. Any seed has the potential to create sprouts, but once the diseased seedlings are burned, then they no longer have that potency. Even though the conceptual confusion is accidental, once eradicated it does not have the potency to regerminate. It cannot reappear."

Shamatha Meditation

As part of the practice of the Dzogchen tradition, the individual should become familiar with shamatha meditation, the meditation of tranquility. Different methods are involved with shamatha meditation. According to the Shravakayana,[32] the practitioner deals with settling the mind by using the meditative gaze. In the Mahayana, the method used by the bodhisattvas places the emphasis on maintaining the stability of the mind. In that context, there is a specific type of meditative gaze involved. Then there is the tantric method, which involves an element of ferocity in relation to the meditative gaze,[33] and the intended goal is to liberate the stability of the mind.

In the context of shamatha, or the meditation of tranquility, the practitioner needs to be aware of the physical posture, and become familiar with the breath. When dealing with the breath, one may analyze the color and shape of the breath, or it may require a focus on counting the breath. Alternatively, one may simply pay attention to the movement of the breath in terms of exhalation and inhalation. Finally, the breathing exercise may involve the practice of the vase-breathing method. Many techniques can be employed with breathing exercises, but the fundamental point is to enable the meditator to achieve a stable mind. One may engage in the practice of shamatha in varieties of ways—there is shamatha that involves signs, and meditation that is devoid of signs. Whatever method is used, the goal of the practice is to settle the mind so that varieties of conceptual proliferation begin to subside, thereby attaining a level of one-pointed concentration.

At the beginning when one's mind is unruly and out of control, the meditator is able to distinguish that state of mind from the meditative state of tranquility. Secondly, when the mind becomes more stable, more focused, then one becomes familiar with the stability aspect of meditation. Thirdly, due to practice one is able to realize *samadhi* or meditative equipoise. Finally, one has not only been able to achieve meditative equipoise, but is able to become autonomous, whereby nothing that occurs in the mind is able to sway or disturb it.

The meditative states that a practitioner may go through are described in different ways in meditation literature. In Mahamudra manuals particularly, it is said that at the beginning of shamatha meditation, the flow of thoughts and concepts is comparable to a waterfall. That waterfall turns into the gentle flow of a river, and finally the mental state becomes comparable to the stillness of the ocean. When the Dzogchen teachings place an emphasis on resting the mind in its natural state or settling the mind in a joyous state, these are comparable to descriptions given in the teachings of Mahamudra and other teachings.

The method a practitioner should employ is relative to the specific needs of the individual. Certain practitioners may require instructions geared toward spontaneous realization, whereas others are given instructions with the graduated path in mind. Individuals do not all have the same capacity, and are not in possession of the same level of intelligence—some are dull, some are average, and there are those of superior intellect. For this reason it is important that the meditation instructor be in tune with the needs and requirements of the individual practitioner, because the instructions given have to correspond to the predilections of that practitioner.

Vipashyana Meditation

Learning to settle the mind through shamatha practice is not sufficient if one is to develop spiritually; one needs to go beyond the stability of the mind, liberating that and not becoming fixated or stuck, which is the purpose of vipashyana meditation.

When discussing vipashyana or the meditation of insight, the stability aspect of the mind has to be realized as the ornamentation of the mind, and the unceasing mental activities that occur in the mind should be perceived as the play of the mind. Finally, the non-duality of these two states of mind, the stable or passive mental state, and the active mental state, should be equalized through this realization. Through vipashyana methods, one's experience is examined in relation to the external phenomenal world. The internal workings of the mind also have to be examined, to come to a point where one realizes that the experience of the external world and the internal workings of the mind are intimately linked, because these two different forms of experience occur in the same mind.

Having engaged in these various vipashyana exercises, the practitioner, first of all, has an experience of recognition, and that is followed by complete certainty in what has been experienced. This series of experiences then culminates in self-liberation. The real essence of vipashyana meditation from the Dzogchen point of view is embodied in this, in relation to the three-step approach to insight meditation. The nature of the mind is completely devoid of empirical characteristics of "thinghood," for the simple reason that the nature of the mind cannot be described as having a certain shape, magnitude, density, or as having this color or that color—it cannot be adequately described. The nature of the mind is emptiness because it is not in possession of attributes and characteristics. While remaining empty of substance, essence, and being devoid of characteristics, it manifests as self-awareness or rigpa—undiluted, non-vitiated, naked awareness.

Recognizing that, having gone through the three steps of vipashyana experience and having come face-to-face with naked awareness is to have authentic realization of one's true condition. This experience is the same as realizing vipashyana meditation, which is nothing other than that. In Dzogchen teachings, this experience is described as "the wisdom expression of Samantabhadra." In this context, Samantabhadra symbolizes that which is unconditioned, and has been so from the very beginning. Kadag means "originally uncorrupted," "originally pure," which is the existential condition of the individual. To realize Samantabhadra is to come to recognize oneself, because finally one has been introduced to one's true condition, a condition which in itself is unconditioned and free from defilement.

If this state is attained, then even when the sensory organs are active and receptive to the visual, audial, nasal, tactile, and gustatory sensory inputs, and when the mind itself is engaged in thoughts involving concepts and ideas, even to the point where judgments are being made in relation to ethics or aesthetics, such as "This is good, that is bad, this is beautiful, that is ugly"—still, the mind does not become disturbed. The mind does not have to manipulate the external world or the way it presents itself, nor is one afflicted with grasping onto things that are considered or judged to be good or bad. The practitioner is not concerned with the notion that things need to be rejected absolutely, or accepted and taken on board in an absolute manner, because there is an experience of real spaciousness. When the undiluted, unadorned, non-vitiated rigpa or self-awareness is realized, that is not different from what is described in Mahayana literature as the "self-originating wisdom of the dharmakaya." Real conviction is born in the individual through this realization.

The tantric visualization practices correspond to vipashyana or insight meditation. The stability aspect of the deity visualization practice comes from focusing the mind on the deity—the shape, the color and the implements being held. The vipashyana aspect comes from realizing that this is a creation of one's mind; the nature of the deity is emptiness. The practice goes beyond attaining stability, but the element of stability needs to be present. In the context of Dzogchen, if vipashyana is practiced without stability, then insight is not possible. On the other hand, with awareness it does not matter what is going on in the mind, there is freedom. Insight does not mean one no longer has to think or judge; to live in the world one has to do all those things. We have to judge, but it is without the presence of clinging. "Dzinpa" means "clinging" and it is a very important word in this context. By letting go of clinging, even if one is making judgments, the spaciousness of the mind is not disrupted. It is hard to become dogmatic or extremist with that underlying spaciousness.

Attainment of samadhi is not really the aim. It does not matter if samadhi or meditative equipoise has been attained or not; that is not the goal. The goal is to employ the stability of the mind that the practitioner has attained through the practice of shamatha, and use that in the context of vipashyana. With that level of stability and vipashyana insight into the spaciousness of the nature of the mind, nothing that is experienced will disturb it.

Vipashyana practice is part of both Dzogchen and Mahamudra, and of all the other Buddhist traditions. The difference lies in how the vipashyana practice is understood. In Dzogchen and Mahamudra, the emphasis is on seeing the nature of the mind itself as being pure. Even though the practice is important, the aim is to go straight into the state of the mind of enlightenment rather than seeing it as a gradual thing. As Dzogchen teachings say, it is kadag, primordially pure, from the beginning. Mahamudra teachings say the same thing, although they do not use the word kadag—the nature of the mind has been pure from the very beginning. There is the idea that one can have direct access straight away, and that is what vipashyana is about in this context.

Usually vipashyana means "the realization of the ultimate condition of things, both in terms of oneself as an individual, and in terms of external reality." That is the understanding of vipashyana that goes across both Dzogchen and Mahamudra traditions.

When it comes to the practice of vipashyana, the nature of the mind itself has to be perceived as manifesting as the adornment of the mind. The various unceasing activities of the mind, which are the thoughts, concepts, ideas, and emotions, are seen as the play of the mind.

Non-duality

Finally comes the mystical realization of the non-duality of the two. There is no duality between the nature of the mind, which manifests as the adornment, and the unceasing mental activities experienced by the individual as thoughts, concepts, ideas, and emotions. These two aspects of the mind are equalized, rendered into a state of equality or neutrality, due to non-dualistic perception.

For that reason, various methods are used in Dzogchen teachings to introduce the practitioner to the external world, so the individual has some appreciation of the real nature of external reality. This affords the student a proper perspective or view of the external phenomenal world. Following that, the inner workings of the mind are introduced through rigpa, self-existing awareness.

From this perspective, the external phenomenal world and the inner workings of the mind are not perceived as separate, existing independently of each other. The final introduction of the mind comes from realizing the non-duality of what is internal, the mind, and what is external, the phenomenal world.

Many different methods are used in Dzogchen teachings to introduce students to this realization: the correct understanding of the external world, the internal workings of the mind, and the non-duality of these two. In this case, the practitioner can understand that the nature of the mind—how the mind itself exists, meaning the existential condition—is realized as being as it is, nothing more, free from conceptions. Furthermore, the nature of the mind is seen as non-substantial; therefore it generates complete conviction. All the activities of the mind, whatever arises in the mind, has the potential to be self-liberated. These three points embody the essentials of vipashyana practice from the Dzogchen point of view.

The nature of the mind is beyond description and beyond attributes or characteristics such as shape or color, precisely because the nature of the mind is emptiness itself, yet at the same time it is awareness. The nature of the mind reveals itself as being both non-substantial and luminous, aware. It is self-cognizing awareness, beyond conceptual categories.

From the Dzogchen point of view, vipashyana experience comes from recognizing that very naked awareness, an awareness not diluted by delusions and distractions. This is the view of vipashyana teachings generally. When the existential condition of the nature of the mind is recognized, that is vipashyana, and all Buddhist traditions agree to an extent upon that point.

Specifically from the Dzogchen point of view, the vipashyana experience has to do with the realization of Samantabhadra, representing the non-vitiated experience of wisdom. The wisdom inherent within one's being from the very beginning is primordially pure, and has existed in conformity with one's existential condition. To know that, to realize that is to realize vipashyana, from the Dzogchen point of view.

Kadag means that it has been pure from the very beginning. *Ka* is the first word in the Tibetan alphabet and *dag* means "pure." So the non-diluted wisdom has been pure from the very beginning. The pure non-diluted wisdom is in conformity, and has always been in conformity with one's existential condition. To experience that is to recognize that the real introduction of the mind has taken place, which is like introducing one person to another.

If this experience has occurred, if rigpa has been realized, and the self-existing awareness has become part of one's daily experience, then it does not matter what the individual goes through, whether it is experienced through the sensory impressions or through being in a state of meditative awareness. At this point it does not even matter what thoughts and ideas are entertained by the meditator. Then why is it that the meditator's experience of these impressions is different from a normal person, who is also subject to these experiences? That is because the meditator is not conditioned by the object of sensory impressions from without, and the mind is not disturbed from within because of grasping. Since the meditator is not swayed by excessive thoughts of acceptance or rejection, they are able to remain in a state of awareness while these mental activities are taking place. The meditator does not deviate from the state of dharmakaya, which is synonymous with self-originating awareness. The recognition of this fact is realized through vipashyana.

Internally, clinging and grasping no longer pollute, vitiate, or corrupt, and thoughts of good and bad, of abandoning and cultivating do not occur or come into play. Beyond that, what is left is undiluted, pure self-awareness, naked awareness. To recognize that is just like recognizing a lost friend. It is recognizing that awareness to be no different from dharmakaya, which is the same as wisdom. To have complete confidence in that is to realize vipashyana from the Dzogchen point of view.

Viewing Mental Events

From the perspective of Dzogchen, there are three ways for the meditator to look at mental events and the varieties of conceptual proliferation that continue to manifest in the state of consciousness.

Firstly, what is the origin of mental events and conceptual proliferation? The origin of mental activities is found in the state of dharmadhatu, in ultimate reality.

At this present moment, where do those mental activities occur? They do not occur outside of dharmadhatu.

The meditator begins to realize that these various mental activities are expressions of or the play of the ultimate reality itself.

Finally, these very activities of the mind become dissipated into nothing other than the actual condition of the ultimate reality.

So whatever arises in relation to the mind itself is sems, or mental events. All those experiences, the conceptual proliferation and everything that arises, from the very beginning, are expressions of dharmadhatu itself. Even the present experiences that one endures should be seen as the self-expression of the dharmadhatu. Finally, the mental activities begin to dissolve into the natural condition of dharmadhatu. Whatever experience arises in the meditator's mind in terms of the beginning, the middle, and the end—those experiences will never deviate from the ultimate authentic condition. It cannot be otherwise.

In this way, the meditator is no longer bound by a linear concept of time, because one is not preoccupied with the past, present, or future. In fact, the Dzogchen meditator does not become liberated but rather realizes that they can remain in a state of naturalness, and a fundamental sense of conviction is established through the experience. The Dzogchen practitioner is free from the concept of the three times—of temporality. One does not become liberated from them, and nor is one bound by them, and one is able to establish full confidence in that experience.

In brief, the nature of the mind manifests in varieties of ways. Sometimes it expresses itself as stable and composed, and at other times it is agitated, disturbed. In the context of Dzogchen meditation, the meditator should not entertain thoughts of good and evil. The meditator should not think of the stable mind as being good and the disturbed mind as being evil, but whatever comes up in the mind should be looked at in its nakedness. To be able to do that is the essence of the trekcho practice of the Dzogchen tradition. Anyone familiar with this approach will not encounter problems with the practice of meditation.

There is no need to fixate on the practice of meditation, where one tries with great effort to remain in the state of meditation. At the same time, the meditator's mind is free of attachment to dualistic notions of the object of experience, and the subject having those experiences. In this particular context, there is no need to use the conventional method of mindfulness practice.

There is no thought of meditation or not meditation, or anything, just simply being aware. According to this type of meditation, even the thoughts and emotions that arise in the mind are not viewed as objects to focus the mind on; they become part of oneself. They are not projected outward and then focused on. Instead, the act of awareness and whatever arises in the mind become merged. It is simply a matter of trying to maintain awareness and not thinking, "Am I aware of them or not?"

No extra effort needs to be made toward the object of

meditation. It is not necessary to exert great effort and suffer hardship in the application of mindfulness toward the object and subject. All those things are not necessary once one has recognized rigpa. Although it is possible that the mind may wander, the ordinary wanderings, delusions and illusions do not have a dwelling-place. One always remains in a state of meditation—that is never deviated from, because of rigpa.

The Meditation Practice

Nowadays most so-called meditation masters have failed to comprehend this point. When they have attained a certain level of shamatha, of mental quiescence, either the meditator is in that state, or too busy observing the unceasing activities of the mind, or constantly following the modulations of the thoughts. Finally, they become caught up with their own fabricated version of the meditative state.

These people have become deceived due to their practice. There are many meditation masters of this kind, and so it is very important that the practitioner gains real confidence in the teachings presented in this text. There are very few people who can appreciate and place confidence in this kind of meditation.

The Dzogchen text, *Tantra of the Garuda in Mid-flight*, elaborates on this point. The Garuda is a mythical bird which unlike other birds is reputed to remain in space and then descend downward. Other birds ascend into the sky, but the Garuda actually comes from above and connects with the earth. Symbolically the Garuda represents rigpa or self-existing awareness.

Real meditation comes from not making the effort to meditate. When awareness is maintained, and one is not preoccupied with sensory impressions and the inner workings of the mind, let the mind rest in its own natural state. Then there is no need to reject one's experiences.

What is the point of conditioning or contriving the mind? There is no need for it. By not conditioning or contriving the mind, it settles into its own condition and nothing needs to be prevented or rejected. It is naturally purified, naturally liberated.

The following quotation is also taken from *The Garuda in Mid-flight*:

The self-existing awareness does not manifest as being this or that. For that reason its nature is emptiness. When the meditator does not firmly hang onto the mental activities or allow themselves to be open to distraction, but lets the mind rest unchanged in its natural state devoid of mental contrivance and deliberate effort, it is self-liberated.

The ignorant, childlike sentient beings cling onto the body, the mind, and conflicting emotions, as if all three possess some enduring essence. However, an advanced practitioner is not preoccupied with these notions, for the simple reason that the yogi does not try to settle the mind in this or that way, does not condition the mind, but remains in the state of awareness, self-existing awareness. Such a practitioner recognizes that the mind has been free of all external influences from the very beginning. For that reason, no one can make it free. When the mind is left to itself in its natural condition, then no effort is necessary.

Numerous texts support this viewpoint and can be cited, but that would be meaningless if the reader was unable to engage in the practice of meditation and have some immediate experience of rigpa or self-existing awareness. One could go on and on with explanations using words and letters, but getting caught up in that would not lead the individual to enlightenment in this lifetime, which is the aim of the practice of Dzogchen. Speculation of all sorts needs to be put aside. The practitioner should concentrate more on the immediate instructions and blessings received from the teacher in order to arrive at some form of certainty within themselves through the practice, so that whatever has been heard or read is internalized. Everything has been taken on board and been made part of oneself.

If that is achieved, then the practitioner no longer needs to worry too much about whether they are practising shamatha, the meditation of tranquility, or vipashyana, the meditation of insight. These two experiences would become united due to the natural unfolding of the meditative experience itself. Shamatha and vipashyana are experienced as being in complete harmony and unity. The meditator no longer concerns themselves with ideas of meditative equipoise during meditation, and post-meditation experiences in everyday life. The experience of awareness, which one has been able to have some intimation of during practice is integrated on all levels of one's experience.

While the meditator is engaged in so-called meditation, they are not disturbed by the goings-on in the mind. Whether the mind is settled in a state of tranquility or there are unceasing mental activities occurring, one does not discriminate between these two states of the mind. The movement or agitation of the mind is not prevented from arising, and the stable, tranquil state of the mind is not deliberately cultivated. Therefore, the meditator is able to enter into the natural state of the mind almost automatically, because to be concerned about stability or agitation is to fall into extreme states of mind. One is free of these extremes.

When the practitioner continues with meditation and tries to sustain development of their experience, temptation may arise regarding those very experiences. If positive experiences come into being that are blissful, enjoyable, and uplifting, then it is very easy for the meditator to fall victim to these experiences. The meditator should not get caught up in the experience itself, but try to remain in, or maintain the meditative ground. If possible, one should divest oneself of thoughts of fruition, of enlightenment, of the goal as a fixed concept, and even of the methods employed on the way, not always being hopeful that everything will turn out all right at the end. Instead, one should realize that the fundamental resources necessary to achieve whatever goal one aims for are already present within. To have that attitude is essentially what the practice of trekcho or cutting through means in the Dzogchen tradition.

Dzogchen, being the pinnacle of all yanas or spiritual vehicles, embodies that attitude. If that understanding is cultivated, then it is not possible to lose what one has achieved with the practice of meditation, nor wander off the course of spiritual development. Everything that is experienced, both good and bad, wholesome and unwholesome, and the varieties of judgments one makes would be revealed as the expression of one's authentic condition, and nothing exists outside of that.

In order to make this point, Garab Dorje,[34] one of the most famous and also one of the most ancient of Dzogchen masters, has this to say:

> The self-existing awareness, which is rigpa, is not something that can be established to exist as this and that, as we do with material things. However, as reflections of that awareness, the individual endures varieties of experiences which manifest in an unceasing manner. Whatever arises in the mind is the reflection of rigpa. For that reason, even the concepts of samsara and nirvana, or bondage and liberation, are expressed as facets of the authentic condition itself. As soon as concepts arise they dissipate into their own natural condition.

The Four Stages of Meditative Experience

A person of superior intellect has the ability to enter into the natural state of the mind directly, but that is not possible for most people. Therefore, the practitioner must engage in the rigorous practice of meditation as presented in the teachings of Dzogchen, and particularly as revealed in the section of Dzogchen known as semde in Tibetan, which literally means "teachings that deal with the mind."

The Dzogchen teachings are divided into three divisions:
The division that deals with the mind (Tib. *semde*)
The nature of the ultimate reality (Tib. *longde*)
Spiritual instructions (Tib. *mennagde*)

In this context, the Dzogchen teachings belonging to the semde division will be compared to the Four Yogas of Mahamudra. In the Dzogchen teachings, the word for "yoga" is not used, but these levels are referred to as "the four stages of meditative experience."

One-pointedness

Having embarked on the path and having had some success with meditation, the practitioner begins to notice just how active the mind is and how thoughts and emotions are being constantly generated. At that point, the meditator does not interpret that experience as being a distraction, but rather recognizes it as part of the meditation process itself. The flow of thoughts is compared to the gentle movement of a river. In due course, the thoughts begin to become more settled and steady.

According to the teachings of Mahamudra, this is seen as the first sign of procurement of the yoga of one-pointedness. It is only the initial stage that has been secured, and for this reason it is referred to as "small one-pointedness." At this stage, the experience of shamatha or the meditation of tranquility, predominates. As the meditator becomes more skilled and experienced, the awareness aspect of the meditation becomes heightened and fostered through practice. Therefore, the element of vipashyana or insight meditation, begins to play a much more important or significant part in the practice. When that happens, the practitioner traverses the last two stages of one-pointedness, namely the middling, and then the final stage of one-pointedness. At this stage, such a meditator may have the experience of psychic phenomena. In post-meditation situations, if the meditator has been able to practice in a legitimate way, one would be able to see all post-meditative experiences as illusory-like. If the meditator has not developed their practice properly, or has not paid sufficient attention during meditation, then in post-meditation, they will continue to be fixated on the experiences and solidify them.

In comparison, the Dzogchen teachings do not speak about "three levels of one-pointedness," or anything of the sort. They focus more on the idea of settling the mind, where the mind is not constantly running wild, reaching out and grasping onto this and that. If the mind is able to settle, then one-pointedness has been realized. Instead of speaking about small, middling, and great one-pointedness, Dzogchen teachings concentrate more on the idea of familiarizing oneself with the mind, increasing that familiarity, and finally, actualizing that. If the practitioner continues to persevere with one-pointedness in this way as a result of their own interest and the teacher's instructions, at times the meditator may be left speechless, in the sense that they cannot express themselves fully through the use of words. Nonetheless, the confidence in meditation has increased.

Simplicity

At this point, the practitioner begins to realize that there is no one wandering in samsara. There is no one bound by delusions and ignorance on the one hand, and no one who has found liberation and the state of nirvana, on the other. This is for the simple reason that such an individual comes to realize that the fundamental source of liberation has existed within, from the very beginning, in the form of dharmakaya, the authentic state of buddha's being. At times, one may develop an enormous feeling of compassion toward sentient beings who have not realized this, and who still continue to suffer due to their ignorance and lack of recognition of this fact. In brief, it means that whatever arises in the mind is seen as an expression of the ultimate reality, which is emptiness.

This realization corresponds to what the Mahamudra teachings mean by "the stage of non-conceptuality or simplicity." Someone at the state of one-pointedness may have this kind of experience, but the difference is that here it is more an understanding than an experience, and it is equated with "small simplicity"or non-conceptuality. Mahamudra teachers sound a warning in relation to this stage of practice. If the practice of mindfulness and awareness is not executed properly, if no mental disturbance occurs, the meditator's mind might go into a state of lethargy. Such a state of mind would have to be seen as defective, because one has entered into the state of relaxation of shamatha, or meditation of tranquility.

The Dzogchen teachings however, advise the meditator not to be too concerned about such things. What is important is to focus on awareness. If awareness is present, one will not get side-tracked and become confused. The fundamental point in this context is to become more and more intimate with the experience of emptiness, or the ultimate reality. Whatever thoughts, emotions, and experiences one may have had in the past that were seen as being substantial and real are now seen as lacking in enduring substance. Not only is this realized on a day-to-day level, but one is able to extend the understanding in relation to more fundamental questions of birth, death, and the intermediate stage, known as the *bardo*. When the individual has extended the understanding of emptiness to such an extent that it encompasses the whole of one's existence, then they arrive at the second stage or middling level of non-conceptuality.

As the practitioner continues, gradually they are no longer disturbed by the manifestation of thoughts, nor pleased by not having them. At this point, the practitioner does not think of thoughts and emotions as something to be discarded, and the methods used to control them as being good. Automatically, everything that occurs in the mind falls into line with mindfulness. One is not overjoyed by what the experience of meditation produces, and when not meditating, one does not feel afraid that one may become distracted. In fact, when the final stage of non-conceptuality or simplicity is achieved, the practitioner is able to be aware of their dreams while asleep. It has to be remembered that the practitioner of non-conceptuality would be very occupied with the idea of emptiness. That person should be forewarned that if they are not in contact with a teacher, then they may begin to think that because everything is imbued with the same reality, then "everything is emptiness and therefore nothing matters." No regard may be shown for the cause and effect of karma, and moral responsibilities may be put aside, because the person no longer thinks that karmic causality is of any significance. The Mahamudra teachings say that it is extremely important not to fall prey to this diversion.

According to the Dzogchen teachings, on the level of simplicity, the meditator has to remain in the state of equanimity where one is no longer concerned about and disturbed by mental lethargy and agitation. They call this "the experience of non-wavering samadhi." Dzogchenpas do not divide this experience into stages as the Mahamudra tradition does, but they again speak about familiarization. How one becomes familiarized with this practice is the same as before, in relation to the stage of one-pointedness.

One-taste

Persevering with the practice, and not falling victim to emotional conflict and conceptual confusion on the one hand, or becoming distracted on the other, the practitioner is able to stay on track. When this practice is pursued further, an experience known as "dissolution of the phenomena into the depth of consciousness" will follow. This means that for the first time, the practitioner is no longer entertaining dualistic thoughts of the object as the apprehended, and the subject as the apprehender. This dualistic notion dissipates into the authentic state of one's being, which is not different from the nature of the mind. Tsele Natsok Rangdrol has made the point that the practitioner may have experiences of extrasensory perception. This initial recognition of non-dualism is an indication of one's understanding of the ultimate reality, which is emptiness. The practitioner is no longer disturbed by notions of causes and conditions, both internal and external, and the effects thereof. The practitioner realizes that causes, conditions, effects, and the interrelationship between these three is what sustains the empirical world. To realize that is the same as having an experience of the small stage of one-taste in Mahamudra.

As the meditation progresses and the meditator becomes more skilled with the practice, one is more in command of what is going on in the mind, rather than falling victim to the various experiences that arise from the mind. At the same time, the meditator is no longer vulnerable to the distraction of external sensory impressions. The reason one is able to come to this point of development is due to the increased ability developed in relation to mindfulness. However, because of the storehouse consciousness, which is the reservoir of all our mental habits, at this stage of development, the meditator may occasionally have certain experiences due to their unconscious mental dispositions. From time to time, delusions may arise, but having become firmly established in the practice of mindfulness, one is no longer swayed by the inner workings of the mind or the external distractions from sensory impressions. In terms of understanding the relationship between causes, conditions, and effects, that understanding has matured further and is clearer and more translucent. This is referred to as "the second stage of one-taste."

In relation to this stage of development, it is said that the meditator is either practicing according to the stage of simplicity, or the stage of one-taste, which follows. If meditation is practiced without focusing on emptiness, but relying on mindfulness alone, then that is the experience of simplicity. However, if that experience is accompanied by an understanding of emptiness, then that is one-taste. At this point, there is still a distinction between meditation and post-meditation experiences, and that is accepted by both Mahamudra teachers and Dzogchen masters. While in a state of meditation, at this stage, one realizes that the experiences of samsara and nirvana have the same taste in relation to ultimate reality. The meditative experience is space-like.

In post-meditation, the meditator realizes that everything is the play of the mind. All that is experienced and encountered is part of the play of the mind, therefore one becomes fearless and develops complete confidence. When the practitioner arrives at this stage of realization, then the superior level of one-taste has been secured.

Some meditation masters have said that at this point there is not much distinction between meditation and post-meditation; they mingle. However, there is some definition between these two states. Most masters belonging to the two traditions agree that at this level there is a slight difference in terms of meditation and post-meditation states. Even at this stage, it has to be remembered that one is not fully free of unconscious tendencies, because subtle thoughts related to the notion of subject and object may still persist. These are subtle forms of dualism, and are not apparent or manifest. Furthermore, the meditator has complete control over the relationship between causes, conditions, and their effects—this is the great one-taste.

Non-Meditation

From this point onwards, it is possible that some individuals may achieve enlightenment during the bardo or intermediate stage, if they have not been able to achieve enlightenment in their lifetime. Tsele Natsok Rangdrol says that in this day and age, it is very rare for people to go beyond the experience of one-taste in their lifetime. However, if individuals want to pursue the practice with great diligence, then the onset of the next stage is quite pronounced due to recognition of the very conscious experience one has where there is no distinction between meditation and post-meditation experiences. However, maintaining that sense of mindfulness and awareness, where one is not applying mindfulness and awareness in relation to any particular object, means there is no object of mindfulness or awareness to use in order to enhance and foster the meditation. That is the small stage of non-meditation.

While perception of the external world and the inner workings of the mind may continue, all the mental activities that are experienced become self-liberated instead of providing further psychic impressions and reinforcing habitual patterns. In Mahamudra teachings, this experience is known as "the meeting of the mother and son luminosities," and it corresponds to the second level of non-meditation, the middling non-meditation. As this particular practice becomes perfected, all thoughts of "object" in the phenomenal world, and "subject" as the apprehender, are exhausted. Even the thought of mindfulness and awareness is transcended, because one's own mind has become that of the buddha. This stage is known as "the great non-meditation."

According to Dzogchen, this experience is referred to as "spontaneous presence" or "spontaneous experience," where there is no longer any notion of meditation or non-meditation. The result of this experience is that there is no fixation on concepts and ideas. Meditation is no longer disrupted; it is a continuous process.

In brief, among the four types of experiences that Dzogchen

teachers speak about, and the Four Yogas of Mahamudra that Mahamudra meditators emphasize, there is a lot of agreement. There is congruence between these two sets of teachings, and that is borne out by the general agreement that exists between the masters of these two traditions. Tsele Natsok Rangdrol comments: "As for myself, I do not have the experience or realization to have certainty in terms of what I have said, however past masters such as Yongdzin Lodro Gyaltsen[35] have made this point repeatedly, and I have just written what I know from their writings."

Comparison between Mahamudra and Dzogchen

Generally speaking, there is no fundamental difference between Dzogchen and Mahamudra, but they do differ in terms of specifics. There is a difference between whether phenomenal experience can be said to be dependent on the mind, whether delusions are identified with the authentic state of buddha's being or dharmakaya, or whether one should rely on mindfulness. When the differences between these two approaches have been pursued, then occasionally, one tradition has criticized the other for various reasons. For example, Mahamudra teachers have criticized Dzogchen teachers for not emphasizing mindfulness enough, where instead the mind is said to be allowed to disappear into the nature of the mind.

On the other hand, Dzogchenpas have felt that Mahamudra teachings rely too much on the graduated path and on thoughts and concepts. So there are certain differences in terms of the approach, but for those who are serious about the practice and have some meditative experience and understanding of what is involved, then everything that is experienced is an expression of the authentic state of being, which is dharmakaya; there are no distinctions. In this way it is possible to resolve the differences.

When Mahamudra teachers claim that Dzogchenpas emphasize the nature of the mind too much where in practice the mind is allowed to disappear into the state of its original awareness, then we have to remember that when Dzogchen teachers speak about the authentic state of being, that is not different from the sutric concept of buddha-nature. In any case, in the teachings of Mahamudra, numerous references are made to this way of being, such as "ground Mahamudra" or "the natural state of being of Mahamudra." Both traditions use various methods for realizing that very state. In fact, these methods are not very different at all. So Mahamudra practitioners cannot find fault with Dzogchenpas for deviating from the correct course of meditation practice.

By the same token, when Mahamudra followers and teachers are criticized for being fixated on the view, which is conceptual, then it has to be realized that that criticism only holds true for the very few people hanging onto the idea of Mahamudra in that conceptual way. To someone who has fully realized Mahamudrahood or its significance, who realizes that the natural state of the mind is something beyond thoughts and concepts, where one comes face-to-face with one's own original face, then there are no concepts, so it cannot be corrupted by concepts.

Dzogchenpas claim that Mahamudra followers identify their delusory thoughts with dharmakaya, or the authentic state of being. That is based upon misunderstanding. Mahamudra followers would not say that ordinary deluded thoughts are the dharmakaya. However, both Mahamudra and Dzogchen understand that each thought and emotion as it arises, if recognized properly, is the expression of one's own natural state of being. Even Dzogchenpas recommend the method of not preventing thoughts from arising in the mind, so there is that agreement.

As for whether the phenomenal world has intrinsic reality or not, from the ultimate point of view, the two traditions come to the same conclusion, because from this vantage point, nothing can be said to be intrinsically true or false. The nature of the phenomenal world is transcendent, even though on the relative level, one experiences varieties of things uninhibitedly. Whatever experience one has of the phenomenal world is devoid of enduring essence.

The Mahamudra and Dzogchen traditions also have the same understanding in terms of practice, because they both emphasize the importance of not exercising acceptance and rejection. Judgments are not placed upon an experience one may have of the phenomenal world that could consequently lead to a response of acceptance or rejection.

Certain questions are also raised as to whether mindfulness is a genuine form of meditation. In relation to this, all that can be said is that some practitioners of the Mahamudra tradition may have over-emphasized the importance of mindfulness practice, where it is seen as a way of holding firmly onto the object of meditation— and they have mistaken that mindfulness practice for genuine Mahamudra meditation. The fault lies squarely on the shoulders of those misguided practitioners, and not on the system of Mahamudra meditation as a whole, since the great Kagyu masters of the past who were qualified to make pronouncements on these matters have always pointed out that mindfulness practice must be accompanied by awareness.

In that sense. there is no difference between these traditions, because the followers of Dzogchen also stress the importance of rigpa or self-awareness. Even though the Dzogchen teachings generally do not mention the word "mindfulness," nonetheless, it is how mindfulness is practiced that is important. If practiced according to Mahamudra instructions, then these two traditions converge and are not at variance. Neither one advocates that the practice of mindfulness is central to the realization of Mahamudra, or Dzogchen.

Three Aspects of Wisdom

In brief, the Dzogchen system deals with three aspects of wisdom:

The Essence of the mind is original purity.

The Nature of the mind is self-perfection.

Responsiveness is unceasing mental activities.

According to the Mahamudra system:

The original ground is said to be unoriginated.

The reflection of the unoriginated state is unceasing.

The creative activity of the mind can manifest in a variety of
ways.

When discussing the two individual traditions, different
terminology may be used, but in terms of the referent or meaning,
there is no difference. Any difference has to do with semantics—
there is no real disagreement lying at the heart of the two traditions.
As with the stratification of the meditative experiences as presented
previously in relation to the Four Yogas of Mahamudra and the
four meditative experiences of Dzogchen, where the question of
the graduated path and the simultaneous path were alluded to,
here, also, what is at issue is not actually the doctrinal truth of one
system or the other.

Other factors have to be taken into account, because whether a
person makes progress on the spiritual path is not contingent upon
what one believes in. It is dependent upon the level of effort that has
been put in and whether certain spiritual insights have been brought
into and have influenced one's daily life so that the spiritual insight
has an influence there, rather than the other way around where the
preoccupations of daily activities begin to corrupt one's spiritual life.
One's judgment and awareness have to be exercised in a personal way.
It is unwise to cling with absolute dogmatism and on prejudicial
grounds to one doctrinal system as opposed to another.

The practitioner should not become anxious in terms of the meditative experience thinking, "Am I having a good experience, or a bad experience, or no experience at all?" Rather, one should try to rejuvenate and sustain an interest in the practice of meditation with the thought of seeing the masters of these traditions as living buddhas, and have confidence in the things they have spoken about. Secondly, one should have persistence in relation to practice. If there is persistence and real confidence in the teachings and in what one is doing, then doubtless one will be rewarded with both meditative experience and realization. It is impossible that one's efforts will go to waste.

How to Continue the Practice

In this way, the nature of the mind has revealed itself from the beginning to be not different from dharmakaya, the authentic state of one's being. In this context, what is required is that one pays attention without deliberation to whatever arises in the mind. In other words, one does not elaborate upon one's immediate experience. In this case, there is nothing to be meditated upon, precisely for the reason that although generally, conventionally, meditation is seen as focusing the mind on an object of meditation, that is not available here. On the other hand, with this exercise, one does not become submerged in mental confusion and delusion, and therefore does not become lost. What is required in this practice is to try not to condition or contrive the mind in any way, but to create space for the natural expression of the mind while maintaining awareness, self-cognizing awareness.

Numerous sutric and tantric teachings support the view and practice put forward here. Even the sutric teachings do not contradict what the Mahamudra and Dzogchen teachings speak about.

The *Sutra of the Pleasant Night* has this to say:

The meditator should not be retrospective, reliving past experiences during meditation.

Nor should the meditator be prospective, in terms of harboring thoughts of the future with great expectation.

What the meditator should do is pay attention to whatever is occurring at a given moment, without fixation. By doing this, the meditator becomes skilled in the practice of meditation.

Tantric literature makes the same point. The *Tantra of No Letters* says:

By establishing the right view, then whatever sensory impressions one may encounter through the senses will be revealed as expressions of the ultimate reality or dharmadhatu.

If the meditator is not being a busybody, running hither and thither and everywhere, then one finds the place of bliss.

If the meditator is able to directly confront whatever arises in the mind with a sense of friendliness, then whatever arises is seen as one's companion. All problems can be solved with this one single remedy—there is no other remedy required.

Savaripa,[36] one of the most outstanding tantric masters, says:

One should never view one's experiences from a negative vantage point. Whatever is experienced, positive or negative, is not judged. Without judging what is experienced in the mind, awareness should be maintained so that one does not become susceptible to distraction. Furthermore, the meditator should not have an expectation of positive meditative experiences.

Panchen Sakya Shri,[37] a Tibetan master, reinforces this view, saying:

> When you recognize the nature of whatever arises,
> Awareness is liberated in its natural state.
> When those thoughts are apprehended properly,
> Then all notions of mindfulness and understanding dissipate.
> When you cut through the pursuance of thought,
> Your thinking dissolves into dharmadhatu,
> The thoughts dissipate.

In terms of meditation and post-meditation states, mindfulness is maintained.

If one maintains mindfulness between sessions in the correct manner, without contrivance, then one-taste will be realized. There will be no difference between meditation and post-meditation experiences, because mindfulness has been maintained.

According to Chisam Namkha Drak:[38]

> We repeatedly mention that in the practice of meditation there is nothing to meditate on. This means that there is nothing, even of the size of an atom, that can be meditated upon, and the practice of non-meditation does not lead the individual to distraction even for a second.

> For those who have understood the nature of the reality and have recognized it, seen it, then the concepts of meditation or meditator do not arise. For those who are endowed with intellect, distractions will not occur even for a second. This is how a yogi meditates. The yogi meditates in the state of non-meditation, but that state of non-meditation is without distraction. It is non-meditation because the yogi does not deliberately engage in the practice of meditation, and on the other hand, the

yogi is not subject to distraction.

The master known as Kaduk Yagdey Panchen[39] says:

> If one meditates with great deliberation, then that is nothing other than conceptual fabrication. If one has become distracted, then one will be lost in the midst of delusion. To recognize that the very conceptual fabrication one is trying to avoid is not different from awareness is to find liberation.

The master, Nub Ben Yonten Gyatso,[40] explains:

> What is meant by the concept of non-meditation is that when one starts to focus the mind either on the subject as an embodied being with consciousness, or on the objective, external, material world, one begins to realize that neither of these aspects of reality has any essential essence. There is nothing to meditate upon.

> When disturbing thoughts and emotions arise in the mind, then what is required is the recognition that these thoughts and emotions have the same nature as the ultimate reality itself. In this way, this form of meditation is also known as non-meditation, because there is nothing else to meditate upon other than the ultimate reality itself.

> To meditate in any other way requires deliberation and the use of conceptual frameworks.

> When the meditator is engaged in this form of meditation, there is no need to resort to the use of antidotes, or invest enormous energy to prevent certain harmful and negative thoughts and emotions from arising in the mind.

> As such, the meditator is able to remain in the state of unceasing awareness in three segments of time—past, present, and future.

Tsele Natsok Rangdrol makes the point that sufficient authoritative backing for this particular practice has been cited, and there is no need to draw from textual authorities any further.

Thogal—Leaping Over

Having discussed the philosophy and practice of trekcho, which emphasizes the combining of intrinsic awareness, rigpa, and emptiness, this section of the text is concerned with the supreme philosophy and practice of thogal, or leaping over.

The teaching of thogal as opposed to trekcho highlights the importance of the integration between the phenomenal world and emptiness but the author of the text says that this can only be dealt with in a summary manner, and not in detail. In discussing thogal, we are dealing with the concept of leaping over. It has to be acknowledged that we are talking about something of enormous importance, because thogal teachings are not discussed in the Three Cycles of the Dzogchen tradition. The majority of teachings of Dzogchen belong to the Mind Cycle, the Space Cycle, or the Cycle of Spiritual Instructions—semde, longde, and mennagde in Tibetan.

The word "cycle" signifies that the process is more circular, instead of having a beginning and an end. The departure point is the same as the destination, which is what Dzogchen is all about—only illusion separates the departure point from the destination. We have to make the journey, only to discover that we have always been at home.

Since thogal is not discussed directly within the Three Cycles of Dzogchen teachings in the body of the Dzogchen tradition, then obviously there is no need to labor the point by saying that non-Dzogchen teachings have paid no attention to them. Most Tibetan teachers familiar with the renaissance of Buddhism in Tibet[41] do not have the ability to fully comprehend what was presented by the Dzogchen teachers in terms of thogal material.

That does not mean that there are not individuals endowed with the capacity to absorb and assimilate the teachings of thogal, to take everything on board and not deviate from the path. However, when it comes to ordinary human beings, they do not have that capacity, and the criticism regarding who is and who is not capable of understanding thogal teachings is lost. With ordinary human beings who have no interest in spiritual teachings to begin with, there is no need to emphasize the elitist concept of thogal teachings. The point is that many Dzogchen teachers have said that the followers of the teachings of the masters who were part of the Buddhist renaissance did not have the capacity to understand thogal. But it cannot be so clear-cut, and that is the author's point.

The teaching of thogal will be presented in two stages:

The first stage will deal with how the state of one's authentic being exists in itself.

The second stage pertains to how that authentic state becomes realized.

How the State of One's Authentic Being Exists in Itself

As for the first stage, within every sentient creature lies the essence of wakefulness or buddha-nature, which is not different from ultimate reality. In the subjective mode, the inherent wisdom is expressed. This point has been made again and again in relation to the trekcho teachings of cutting through. What it means is that buddha-nature is not to be discovered outside one's mindstream, or stream of consciousness. When the mind rests in the state of luminosity and emptiness, the state of nakedness, that is self-realization, self-recognition, which is the same as understanding buddha-nature.

Where does the luminosity of the mind dwell? The luminosity of the mind dwells in the physical body, and with this understanding, one will come to realize that the physical body is not the ordinary body it is thought to be, but the divine mansion. The luminosity element of the mind, which is rigpa, is encased in the physical body in a self-perfected way.

In what way does the self-cognizing awareness or luminosity of the mind exist? Concepts of time, like the past, present, and future, or ontological concepts of existence or nonexistence cannot be used, because these concepts are not applicable to the reality of the self-existing awareness.

The emptiness nature of the three times, the past, present, and the future, has no intrinsic reality—that is the fourth dimension of time, according to Buddhism. We tend to think that the past exists in its own way, and that the present exists, but none of the three times has intrinsic reality because all three are encompassed in the time of dharmadhatu, or the time of eternity, which is changeless, and does not exist in time.

In itself, self-existing awareness cannot be described or explained, but on the empirical level, the worldly level, it finds its expression through the body, speech, and mind. In that way, self-existing awareness reaches out and pervades all aspects of one's being. Self-existing awareness pervades the physical body, which is the first of the five *skandhas*.[42]

The dwelling-place of self-existing awareness can be found in the midst of *citta* (Skt.), which means "consciousness." In this context, citta should be seen as the luminous palace—the dwelling-place of self-existing awareness.

In what manner does the self-existing awareness dwell? The lamp of self-existing awareness has three characteristics that correspond to the three aspects of buddha's being—dharmakaya, sambhogakaya, and nirmanakaya. In its authentic state, which is dharmakaya, it is free from embellishment and conceptual fabrication. As an expression of sambhogakaya, it manifests as the five lights of wisdom. In terms of responsiveness, which was discussed in connection with trekcho practice, it corresponds to the six senses, as six lamps.

In relation to the six lamps, the thogal teachings emphasize the concept of luminosity. Instead of the senses obstructing the wisdom and resulting in accumulation of a variety of negative thought formations, whatever is seen, heard, touched, smelled, and tasted becomes illuminating, rather than leading to more delusion and increasing ignorance.

The Dzogchen tantra, *Luminous Space*, states:

> Within all sentient creatures is citta, consciousness, along with the bones of the human skeletal arrangement, where the nerves and arteries are the gates or doors, and rigpa, self-existing awareness, exists within them all. Citta, consciousness, and the bones are like the house that encases self-existing awareness, and the nadis, the nerves and arteries, are like the doors.

> This very body is precious because within it lies the self-existing awareness, the embodiment of emptiness and luminosity, and from that arises responsiveness, which is like the illumination obtained from a lamp.

The human body is seen as a whole, with bones, *nadis*, and citta, which in this case is referring to the heart. It is the vase, and within the vase is found self-existing awareness. Just like a lamp placed in the vase, so we have self-existing awareness existing within our body. Rigpa, self-existing awareness, pervades all aspects of one's body and mind, including the senses and the psychophysical constituents. The analogy transcends the mind-body dualism that the body is material, that it is base, terrible, and that the spiritual is superior to the physical. That duality is transcended by realizing that what is most precious, the self-existing awareness, not only dwells in the body but is also in intimate relationship with the body—it pervades all aspects of one's body in terms of its nerves, bones, heart, and sensory organs.

The five Buddha families are represented by one hundred and forty-two wrathful and peaceful deities. They are the expression of one's true identity and have always been present within one's being. This realization does not exist in the mindstreams of normal sentient beings, who are subject to delusion of all kinds regarding themselves and the external world, and distracted by the five psychophysical constituents, the five elements, and the sensory impressions. For the genuine practitioner, these concepts and ideas relating to the physical and mental aspects of one's being are revealed as the relative and absolute aspects of the buddha's physicality and mind.

During the after-death experiences in the postmortem state when visions that are comforting and pleasant, and frightening and repulsive are encountered, the practitioner realizes that all these visions have their origin in the same state. Instead of being caught up in varieties of concepts and ideas, the practitioner begins to understand that ultimately, in terms of fruition, or realization of the spiritual goal, what is to be achieved is not extrinsic to the state of one's being, but intrinsic. The embodiment of buddhahood or the concept of buddha-fields are not extraneous concepts or realities that exist outside the domain of one's being, but they are present within oneself.

Having described how the potentiality for self-fulfilment is already present within one's being, the manner by which that self-recognition or self-realization is achieved needs to be addressed. The methods vary, because within the tantric system, different methods may be introduced. When it comes to personal spiritual instructions, a variety of instructions may be given, due to the differing needs of the practitioners concerned. However we are only concerned about the Dzogchen method as presented in the Three Cycles of Dzogchen—semde, longde, and mennagde.

These Dzogchen teachings reiterate that the concept of tathagatagarbha, or buddha-nature from the sutra teachings, is not different from the nature of the mind, mind-in-itself. The nature of the mind is all-pervasive and present within the mindstreams of all sentient creatures without discrimination, just as the quality of oiliness is present within each sesame seed. The Dzogchen teachings of the Three Cycles concentrate mainly on the practice of trekcho, which has already been discussed. With the Dzogchen teachings of the Cycle of Secret Teachings, the practice of visualization is implemented and the practitioner visualizes the body, hand gestures, and so on of a variety of deities, in keeping with the tantric tradition, particularly in relation to the development stage of tantra.

In relation to the spiritual instructions, four lamps are discussed. Specific methods are introduced to the practitioner in terms of the form, color, and appropriateness of the methods to be employed at any given time. Here, we are fundamentally concerned with the Nyingtik or *Heart Drop* teachings, the essence of Dzogchen teachings.

The Nyingtik teachings include all the varieties and forms of Dzogchen teachings that have been discussed and those teachings correspond to the three aspects of one's being. This is explained very simply in three ways through the use of "meaning," "symbol," and "mark."

At the level of trekcho, three aspects were mentioned, essence, nature, and responsiveness. The teachings of trekcho correspond to the essence aspect of one's being, which relates to meaning. The nature of the mind is luminosity, and that is associated with the

Secret Cycle of the teachings of Dzogchen, which corresponds to symbol. The last type of Dzogchen teachings is related to the Nyingtik or Heart Drop teachings, and that corresponds to the responsiveness aspect of one's being. That is exemplified by mark because here the Nyingtik teachings emphasize the aspect of vision, directly related to the function of the eyes.

If this is not understood, a great deal of confusion can be generated, because the concepts of meaning, symbol, and mark explain how the different teachings of the Dzogchen tradition relate to different aspects of one's being. When that is not understood, individuals with the propensity to indulge in unnecessary philosophical niceties may argue for "this" against "that," and the whole point could be lost in the process. Therefore it is extremely important to adhere to the essential teachings of Nyingtik that emphasize how to immediately develop wisdom and luminosity using specific methods.

The Pathways

First it is appropriate to discuss the tantric concepts of nadi, *bindu, prana*, and *chakra*. Nadi means "energy pathways," bindu means "life-essence," and chakra means "psychic energy center." According to the tantric tradition, there are an infinite number of nadis or energy pathways. In most tantric texts, up to 10 million energy pathways are mentioned. There are about 72 energy pathways that pump blood, and about 260 energy pathways that enhance the flow of prana, meaning "motility," which somewhat resembles oxygen.

Motility is a biological concept used to describe the movement capability of very small micro-organisms. Even if something appears dead and is not breathing, there is still oxygen present and this is the kind of concept that is being spoken about.

Finally, there are about 30 energy pathways involved with the function of life-essence, bindu, which means "bodhicitta."

Bodhicitta in this context does not have the same meaning as it has in Mahayana teachings. Bodhicitta refers here to what can best be described as "life-essence," which has been incorrectly translated as "semen" at times. 37 energy pathways are described in relation to objectivity, and 157 in relation to the function of the five psychic centers of the body. In this context, however, we do not need to be concerned about the details.

The primary concern is the three central energy pathways or channels. Particularly relevant to the Dzogchen teachings is the energy pathway known as "glass tube," the meaning of which will be explained later in the text. The bindu or life-essence is to be understood from two points of view: the relative aspect of the life-essence, which is physical, and the absolute aspect, which is spiritual. What is done or how one deals with the life-essence depends upon the different types of practices. Different methods are used to activate the life-essence, such as visualizing a physical form, a syllable, a circle, light, and so on. It has to be kept in mind that the methods do not conflict but all have the same intention and goal, which is to activate the life-essence, the bodhicitta, or bindu.

In terms of the three central energy pathways, the right pathway has the function of generating bliss, the left produces luminosity, and by uniting these two energies the central one gives rise to non-conceptual experience. When engaged in other forms of tantric practice, the practitioner relies more on the relative, meaning that the focus is on the physical aspect of life-essence. Then there are practices that may be done in relation to the energy pathways and the five psychic energy centers or chakras. Here, however, that is not a concern because one is relying on the more spiritual aspect of life-essence, for the simple reason that the life-essence has the capacity to produce wisdom.

The Lamps

In this context, the practice is performed slightly differently, by visualizing the heart chakra to be of immense importance, and imagining that the citta, the heart, has a type of material coming out of it, comparable to the size of a thread in a white scarf. The thread is split-ended, and this particular energy pathway moves over and joins with the central energy pathway. It goes right through the psychic energy center of the throat, and extends into the cortex where it curves over and drops down into the eyeballs. The thread, which is the energy pathway—the glass tube, as mentioned earlier—is visualized as being white and completely smooth, and is referred to as "the path of wisdom," or "the secret passageway for Vajrasattva," Vajrasattva being the symbol of one's authentic being. When the Nyingtik teachings speak about the transference of consciousness, which is a specific method used at the time of death to eject one's consciousness, this is the same visualization.

The text, *Luminosity of the Ultimate Reality*, states:

> The light of wisdom travels through the energy pathway
> and is hooked up to the visual organs. Through that, one
> is able to experience these four lamps.

The first lamp that the practitioner comes to have experience of is known as the "penetrating water lamp," or "far-reaching water lamp." Through the eye organs the practitioner has direct experience of the authentic state of one's being, which has to do with seeing the world as a buddha-field, and the physical and mental elements as self-arising. The practitioner has direct perception regarding these objects.

The penetrating water lamp has three aspects. The first is the physical basis, the way the eye organs are constructed due to one's physical constitution. It relates to the penetrating sense organ, or far-reaching sense organ. On that physical basis, the second is the cognitive aspect which has to do with the mind, the visual consciousness, known as the "far-reaching power of visual consciousness" or "penetrating visual consciousness." The third aspect, the far-reacher composed of wisdom, is the wisdom that travels through the subtle energy pathway described earlier, but it is quite distinct from the previous two functions of vision. When these three aspects of vision come together and operate in harmony, the individual can have direct experience of ultimate reality or dharmata.

The second lamp is the lamp of pure space. At the beginning, when these shapes appear, they are erratic, always moving. When trying to focus one's eyes on them, because the shapes are moving, one's head and the eye organs might move. What is perceived is very vague and indistinct, but in time these shapes become more stable and distinct. How so? This is because one begins to see these visions in the context of space. The visible manifestation of these images is no longer just in the foreground, but one begins to see them as having a background, a horizon. This is why it is called "the lamp of pure space."

The third lamp is the empty bindu lamp. Bindu literally means "circles," (Tib. *thigle*) so gradually as one progresses, one begins to see circles of light. At the beginning, the circles may be of only one color, but gradually one begins to see multi-colored, five-colored visions of circles. At first, there are only a few, and then they multiply and become more and more colorful. According to Dzogchen teachings, the more colorful they become, the more greatly valued they are. If they assume the colors of a rainbow, they represent one's innate potentiality for wakefulness in relation to the five wisdoms: the five colors of the circles represent one's own five innate wisdoms.

The fourth and final lamp, which is regarded as the most

important one, is called "the lamp of self-existing knowledge." The lamp of self-existing knowledge is no different from the self-awareness that the Dzogchen teachers speak about, no different from rigpa. As the author pointed out, in Dzogchen, there is a significant difference between sems and rigpa. Sems is our ordinary empirical consciousness that thinks, anticipates, remembers, plans, gets worried, becomes anxious, and so on. Rigpa is not like that. Rigpa, or self-existing awareness, is aware of everything that is going on. All of the lamps lead to realization of "the lamp of self-existing knowledge."

The text, *Blazing Light*, says:

> As the unceasing phenomena appear they come in contact with the eye organ, which is endowed with the subtle energy pathway, and wisdom resides within the lotus of the pupil of the eye organ.

It is termed a "lotus," because the dark pupil of the eye is surrounded by the iris, which looks like the petals of a flower.

The *Dra Thalgyur Tantra* says:

> The gate through which the wisdom radiates is the subtle energy pathway. The subtle energy pathway resides in the eye organs and the eye organs act as the gate through which the wisdom shoots forth, because the real wisdom emerges from and through them.

When the practitioner begins to have some understanding of the workings of the three inner lamps of wisdom, then the three outer lamps will automatically become illuminated. The inner ones refer to the subjective aspect, and the outer ones to the objective aspect of the experience.

In addition to the experience of these six lamps, if the person were to die, they would experience the lamp of bardo, the lamp of the intermediate state between birth and death. If the person were to experience the completion stage of Dzogchen, then they would have the experience of the resultant lamp. These would take place automatically. Then there is the lamp of all-pervasiveness, which, being luminous, is inherent within the nature of the mind itself.

In all there are nine expressions of this lamp, however all the different experiences of the lamp can be reduced to six: the three inner lamps and the three outer lamps. When condensed, there are six which can be included within four: the penetrating water lamp, the lamp of pure space, the empty bindu lamp, and the lamp of self-existing knowledge.

How to Realize This Through the Practice

In the previous subsection, three types of inner lamps of wisdom were mentioned. Having understood that, the practitioner should gradually move toward developing real experience in the subsequent illuminations, to make the practice successful. To ensure that what has been experienced is veridical, genuine, authentic, and not delusory, the practitioner should consult with the teacher from time to time to receive instructions, which are like nectar flowing from the mouth of the master. It is essential to establish a proper samaya relationship with the teacher, a genuinely bonding relationship between the student and teacher. The student has the responsibility of not corrupting it, to ensure that this bond remains pure and straightforward. Furthermore, the practitioner should make the effort to go into retreat as frequently as possible. One should spend time in the wilderness where there are no disturbances and where one will not have to deal with unpalatable and disturbing people and situations. However, the practitioner must be in possession of the necessary provisions like food and clothing.

If the practitioner can fulfil these conditions, they will be able to use their body, speech, and mind in the most appropriate manner. Then the body, speech, and mind will not be used in ways harmful to oneself, but in order to understand how samsara, the state of bondage, and nirvana, the state of freedom, can be transcended. In order to do this, the practitioner has to be very sensitive and attentive to the time and place, in terms of engaging in the practices associated with bringing about illumination, or activating the innate lamps, "lamps" being a metaphor for wisdom.

Depending upon the time and place, the meditator may engage in various meditation postures to activate the lamps. To bring about illumination of the authentic state of being, the dharmakaya or *chos sku*, one adopts the posture of a lion.

To activate the sambhogakaya, the illumination arising from the transformed energies of emotional conflict, the meditator adopts the posture of an elephant.

To activate the nirmanakaya, the illumination associated with the unceasing thoughts and concepts and also the physical body itself as an embodiment, the meditator sits in the posture of an ascetic.

In this way, the practitioner must be constantly sensitive to and aware of their conditions, predilections, tendencies, the sort of environment they are living in and so forth, and use their intelligence to determine in what manner they should practice to bring about the necessary and desired goals of the practice, the activation of the inner lamps.

Generally speaking, the practitioner should remain in or try to cultivate a sense of stability, not only in their posture but in the way that the eye movements are used and how the mind works. That is the most fundamental practice involved here, precisely because these three are related. The practitioner must become familiar with the idea of the stability of the body, the eye organs, and the mind.

The Three Essential Points of the Practice

Having emphasized the posture of the body, mind, and the eye organs, there are various methods for how the eye organs should be trained. They are the method of gazing upward, rolling the eyeballs up and thereby aiming at the space; that of gazing downward, rolling the eye organs down and focusing in that way; and the method of rolling the eyeballs sideways. So these are the three ways of training the eye organs in proficiency at gazing or envisioning.

Following from one's training in the practice of gaze there are three kinds of objects to be envisioned. The first is space—one gazes and focuses one's mind into pure space, the cloudless sky, which is the object of the gaze. The second is sunyata, the non-differentiated ground of all beings, or ultimate reality. The third is the self-illuminating aspect of one's mind.

So there are three kinds of envisioning involved, where firstly the eye organs are used, and then the eye organs lead the meditator into having a vision of another kind. To begin with, the practitioner has a vision of something physical, immediately available to the sensory organs, and then due to that, it leads to another form of vision, which is the ultimate reality. That, then is followed by the vision of the aspect of one's own mind, which is self-illuminating.

The dead air should be expelled to begin with—a deep breath is taken in followed by a prolonged exhalation. Having removed the dead air from within one's body, one should proceed to maintaining the stability of the breath, the rhythm of the breath. The meditator should use the awareness they have been able to develop and maintain, so that it is not corrupted and disturbed by superfluous conceptual proliferation, where the mind is led into distraction and delusion. In this way, the meditator should combine the proper rhythm of the breath with awareness. The meditator needs to develop a sense of synchronicity between the two, between the workings of awareness and of the breath. That concludes the three essential points of the practice.

The text, *Thalgyur*, explains:

> For the key points of direct perception, the essential point of the body is not to deviate or disengage from the potentiality of the body, speech, and mind, so that one remains in their continuity. The speech aspect becomes actualized when the meditator can fully appreciate the significance of its potentiality and explicate the profundity of the teachings. The potentiality of the mind becomes actualized when the meditator, having gazed at the external space, comes to understand the nature of the space as ultimate reality. The practitioner should never become separated from these three key points.

In certain texts, the gate, the external world, the flow of psychic energy within the body—which is prana or motility—and rigpa or self-existing awareness, are mentioned in relation to the integration of body, speech, and mind. When the word *sgo*, which means "gate," is mentioned, that refers to the eye organs. In meditation, the eye organs play an important role in bringing the meditator directly into contact with the external world. The eye organs are the gateways to the world. The meditator and the external world, which is the object of the sensory impressions, are then seen as being completely free of embellishment. In other words, the sensory objects reveal themselves as they are. Following that, the psychic energies or prana are properly channeled and the various blockages are overcome, precisely because the psychic energies start to operate in tune with rigpa or self-existing awareness. This results in the development of wisdom.

The importance of coordination of body, speech, and mind is emphasized not only in this text, but in other texts that carry the message of the oral lineage. In the practice involved with ying, which is space—both the external space as we know it and space as the ultimate reality, first the meditator will perceive certain forms of light. This light is endowed with five colors and can appear in varieties of shapes and forms. Circles of light will appear and that is the reason this text is called *The Circle of the Sun*.

At first, the circles of light may appear red, yellow, or orange, and then they become more colorful like the eyes on peacocks' feathers. These circles of light first appear in twos and threes and then multiply to the point where one cannot count the number that have appeared. These self-illuminating circles of lights will appear like a pearl necklace approaching and then distancing itself.

How a practitioner of thogal perceives the lights has much to do with that individual's physical constitution, psychological state, and personality traits. There is no standard way of perceiving the lights. They occur, and the way in which they manifest is conditioned by the individual's predilections and physical constitution.

The tantra, *Blazing Lamp*, says:

> When the eye organs become purified, then the meditator is able to perceive five-colored lights. These five-colored lights gradually start to assume a bluish tinge and all other sensory impressions cease.

and:

> The ultimate reality, which is a form of space, manifests in the form of lights. These lights represent not only the ultimate nature of things, but one's own buddha essence or spiritual spark. This spiritual spark has been present within the mindstream of each sentient being right from the beginning, and is present not only in those beings who are more evolved spiritually, but also in those where the spark has not been ignited. The spark and the space have been in coexistence in a primordial state of union, and this is realized when the spark is ignited and the meditator starts to have visions of five-colored lights and circles of light.

The *Tantra of the Perfected Lion* says:

> The ultimate reality and the illuminating aspect of wisdom are in a continuous relationship. These are not two entities brought together and linked with a third factor, but they merge into each other—they are continuously connected with each other. No third factor has brought these two different things together, and they remain and exist in a state of mutual engagement. When the practitioner realizes this, the self-existing awareness, rigpa, will manifest in the five-colored visions of one's own authentic state. The space, the ultimate reality, and rigpa or self-existing awareness, and the wisdom which the recognition of these two leads to, are the same insofar as there is a continuous relationship between the three. Not that they are exactly the same—they cannot be separated, nor can they merge with each other completely. While retaining its own characteristic, each member of this relationship is also part of the other two.

There are many tantras that make the same point.

When the practitioner realizes the nature of prajna, discriminating awareness, they come into contact with *jnana*, wisdom. This is the key point of trekcho practice, because trekcho practice leads the meditator to direct realization of self-existing awareness, self-cognizing wisdom. The prajna is able to unlock the self-cognizing wisdom. Self-cognizing wisdom is not part of everyday consciousness. It has been made very clear throughout this text that there is a distinction between consciousness, which is sems (Skt. *citta*), and rigpa or self-cognizing wisdom (Skt. *vidya*). There is a difference between sems and rigpa, and to conflate these two concepts can be very misleading.

As the text has made very clear from the outset, there is a major distinction between kadag, primordial purity, and kun gzhi, the basis of one's consciousness, which includes the unconscious. Although those two are fundamental for one's own existence and for life generally, they are different from each other. When engaged in the practices of trekcho and thogal, one must distinguish between sems and rigpa; one should always rely on rigpa, and not on sems, one's ordinary consciousness. The ordinary states of consciousness are the source of the distortion of one's perceptions and of one's erroneous behaviour. Rigpa or vidya is illuminating, and can guide the practitioner on the right path.

The distinction is made between consciousness and rigpa or vidya because the consciousness is very much dependent on one's physical condition, on the workings of the body, such as the circulation of breath. The mind is greatly conditioned by one's nervous system, and the way one exhales and inhales through the nose and the mouth. Because of sems or citta, ordinary consciousness, we suffer varieties of afflictions, both physical and mental. This is the activity aspect of consciousness and its nature is ignorance, because ordinary consciousness is not aware of itself—therefore it is susceptible to various forms of error and distortion.

"Mind," "conceptual activities of the mind," "ordinary mind," and "the ordinary state of consciousness" are synonyms for what is broadly referred to as sems, which is always in motion and never at rest. This movement comes from agitation of the energies within the body—it is because these energies are stirred up that the mind becomes disturbed. In Dzogchen practice, we do not pay much attention to the ordinary state of the mind or the circulation of the energy or prana, because the intention of Dzogchen practice is to go beyond that. For that reason we have concentrated mainly on how to cultivate rigpa, and have discussed this in relation to place, in relation to the path and gateways. Dzogchen practices are about the cultivation of rigpa, not about what the sems is doing or what state it is in.

Having explained how sems or ordinary consciousness, and rigpa are different, then in relation to this, rigpa must be thought of as being quite distinct from sems or the ordinary consciousness that feels, anticipates, and recollects. Unlike the ordinary or everyday consciousness whose synonyms have already been listed, the synonyms used to refer to one's original state or rigpa, are "buddha-nature," "the authentic aspect of being," "the symbolic and manifest aspects of being of the buddha," and "the non-differentiability of the three aspects of buddhahood"—dharmakaya, sambhogakaya, and nirmanakaya.

The function of the two related but distinct aspects of wisdom which are known as the wisdom which apprehends the ultimate reality, and the wisdom which apprehends the nature of all things, is to provide the possibility of liberation and enlightenment—unlike sems, which is seen as the origin of all one's turmoil, frustration, suffering, and misery. Because rigpa is inherent within one's nature, it has the ability to fructify, to bring to fruition the spiritual potentiality for liberation. The fructification of the spiritual potentiality for liberation is made possible because of this element, rigpa—that is part of one's nature.

In Buddhist literature, this element is referred to by many names. Terms such as "original purity," "beyond conceptualization," "self-existing awareness," "dharmakaya" or "the authentic aspect of buddha's being," "perfect circle" or "the essential self-existing circle," "transcendental knowledge," "true wisdom," "Mahamudra," and "Dzogchen," all refer to one's authentic, uncorrupted, natural state of being. The practitioner needs to understand this and not become overly fixated on the various words, terms, and labels.

In thogal teachings, the element existing primordially as part of one's nature is known as "the lamp of self-existing awareness." In relation to the different expressions of wisdom, described as "lamps," that have already been discussed, the main expression of wisdom is the lamp of self-existing awareness, and that is the referent. When a text uses any of those words and terms, it is speaking about this particular experience. It is the same experience; the referent is the same, but the words are different. The lamp of self-existing awareness is the most fundamental lamp, and all the others are its expression. Whether an individual succeeds or not with spiritual practice depends on their ability or lack of it, to apprehend self-existing awareness. All those words and terms refer to that particular way of experiencing, that way of being.

The text, *Blazing Lamp*, elucidates this point:

> This self-existing awareness is the lamp which illuminates everything precisely, because there is only one wisdom that can reveal the nature of all that can be known.
>
> Phenomenal objects, whether they are perceived or not— all these existing things are apprehended as lacking in substantiality and inherent existence. This is the characteristic of self-existing awareness.
>
> Although the cognitive activities of the mind fluctuate, change, and are vulnerable to external influences, nonetheless, if the meditator has been in touch with, or has had a glimpse of self-existing awareness, then when seeing an object, the intellectual or conceptual understanding that follows, and rigpa, self-existing awareness, will be perceived as being in a state of union.

When the practitioner is able to do that, everything will be self-liberated. Whatever has taken place in the mind of that individual becomes self-liberated. The senses, the mind, and the intellect are brought into a state of unity, and self-liberation is made possible. By knowing the lamp of self-existing awareness, then everything else becomes self-liberated. Without it, everything is divided, divisive and conflictual, but when the lamp of self-existing awareness is present, then all things are brought into a state of harmony.

The practices concerned with actualizing self-existing awareness are crucial, not only in relation to thogal experiences, the visions described previously, but also in relation to the workings of the senses and the sense perceptions. The practitioner's psychic dispositions, tendencies, and inclinations are very much connected to this principle of self-existing awareness. Whether one finds liberation through sensation, through the perceptual apparatus, or through one's psychic tendencies or inclinations and dispositional factors, is determined by the presence or absence of self-cognizing awareness. Again, although there are different types or manifestations of the so-called lamps, the real lamp that illuminates is the all-pervading, self-originated, self-existing awareness. This type of awareness is not brought about by something external, whether in its function or its origin. The self-existing awareness makes itself known to the individual as continuous awareness. Self-existing awareness is innate, latent, and its existence can be known only through practice, by focusing the mind on continuous awareness.

The tantric text, *Adornment of Precious Stones*, says:

If the practitioner is interested in gaining insight into the mind of the buddha, then one should focus on the continuous state of awareness in relation to the body.

If the intention is to develop understanding related to the intention of the buddha, one must try not to become separated from continuous awareness.

If the practitioner is interested in expanding their knowledge of the teachings, they should try to understand the way in which the continuous state of awareness rests.

If one desires experience of the unity between meditation,

view, and action, then the practitioner should maintain one-pointedness in relation to the continuous awareness, because continuous awareness is the very embodiment of the qualities of enlightenment, even in its physical form.

In this way, the practitioner of Dzogchen must attempt to combine trekcho and thogal.

The Continuing Practice

In post-meditation situations, during sleep and in waking hours, the mind should not be allowed to wander. During the daytime, without rejecting the functions of the sense perceptions, one should learn to practice self-liberation through perception, through the functions of the six senses. One does not block them out to maintain composure in an effort to stop the mind becoming scattered, nor allow oneself to become distracted so that one is not present and as a result one is swayed by a range of sensory impressions. This practice can be enhanced by thinking, "Whatever I am perceiving through the senses does not have objective enduring essence."

At night, at the time of sleep, instead of allowing the mind to dream, fantasize, or simply drift into a state of sluggishness, the practitioner should try to cultivate awareness so that the luminosity aspect of the mind is activated. Day and night, the practitioner has occasion to make use of every opportunity that presents itself in order to enhance their spiritual progress and develop more insight. The other factor to be taken into account is for the practitioner to avoid being clingy, greedy, and wanting.

The essence of the practice can be condensed into the bringing together of the self-existing awareness or rigpa, and ultimate reality, ying. With the concept of rigpa, self-existing awareness is the primordial rigpa, and then the secondary rigpa, or derived rigpa, comes from the practice of meditation. By becoming more aware, that is rigpa in itself.

Four Key Points to Maintain

1. The view that the Dzogchen practitioner must hold is to bring ying and rigpa together; this is the essence of Dzogchen practice.

2. The meditation is concerned with not separating the phenomenal world and ultimate reality, which is emptiness.

3. The spiritual instruction concerned with this practice is to understand that through gaining more insight into, and becoming closer to rigpa, the practitioner has the ability to strip away all manner of delusion and negative habitual patterns.

4. The fourth and final essential point involved with Dzogchen practice is to allow the sensory impressions of the phenomenal world to be self-liberated through the practice of meditation, so that the mind is no longer susceptible to either excitement and elation; or stupor, drowsiness, and depression.

This is how the Dzogchen practitioner needs to continue with their practice. How to achieve this has been explained, and these four points related to Dzogchen practice have been elaborated on in this text and in many other Dzogchen manuals. To realize that ying and rigpa are inseparable, the first of the above four points, is the goal and the practice of Dzogchen—everything else is subsumed under this particular topic.

How the Signs and Degrees of Progress Manifest

The essential teachings involved with the practice of trekcho are very much in tune with the tradition of Mahamudra, however the text at this point is primarily concerned with the practice of thogal, leaping over. It has already been made known that the practice of thogal has to do with experiencing certain visions.

To summarize, we can discuss the four visions involved with thogal practice, firstly by attempting to explain how the visions manifest and secondly, by discussing the signs of meditational progress that appear or manifest to the meditator.

At this point, the importance of engaging in ngondro, or preliminary practice, needs to be stressed, because it is very easy for the meditator to think that they can go straight to the practice of thogal, bypassing everything. One must be properly grounded in ngondro practice to develop appreciation of the two conditions of the totality of existence, namely samsara and nirvana, the state of bondage and that of liberation. Without being acquainted with the general and more specific practices of ngondro, then even if an individual embarked on the path of Dzogchen and engaged in thogal practice, they would fail to experience the visions and to perceive the signs of progress. Furthermore, the meditator should be alert to the fact that practicing trekcho, which has already been described in some detail in this text, should be used as the ground. Without having a thorough understanding of that, they will not succeed with the practice of thogal. For these reasons, it is important to spend a great deal of time with ngondro practice and the practice of trekcho, trying to follow them without aberration. If the practitioner persists with the practices of ngondro and trekcho, then the visions of thogal would start to manifest.

The Vision of Manifest Dharmata

As the ultimate reality becomes merged with self-existing awareness, then one would experience a kind of vision of light. When the light has intensified, these visions are referred to as "lamps." This section of the text has dealt with the meaning of the visions but here, "lamps" signifies that when the vision of light intensifies and deepens, then certain circles of light develop, known as bindu in Sanskrit, thigle in Tibetan, which finally leads to realization of self-existing awareness.

Three Stages in Relation to the Visions

In relation to the visions, the practitioner would normally go through three stages.

First, there is initial contact with self-existing awareness, but this is unstable and just a momentary, fleeting experience. This experience is likened to "being able to get hold of the rope that is connected to the nose of an animal." If someone has tied a rope to the nose of an animal, then they know that they can lead it by the rope.

This is followed by a deepening of that experience, where it becomes more beneficial and uplifting, and whatever is experienced is seen as enriching and good. In this way, the meditator establishes themselves in the practice. This is the second stage of the visionary experiences involved with thogal. Here, the circles of the sun may manifest.

Finally, the meditator is able to marry and combine the extra-terrestrial and the terrestrial states. The unity of the two is perceived immediately, without effort. This is the final kind of vision, following from attainment of the third stage of thogal experience.

Signs of Progress

In terms of the signs, these are connected with what are known as "the three gates." These signs indicate actualization of one's own true condition.

In relation to the first gate, which is the body, the teachings say that one's body is seen as completely spontaneous and unrestricted, precisely because the body is not put to use for any specified task or project. The body is not assigned a designated task. Because of this, the meditator will have a sense of being with the body in its natural state. Furthermore, if one receives the vase empowerment, then this potentiality of the body becomes actualized. The body is then able to function free from effort or exertion and therefore is spontaneous and natural.

For the second gate, which is the verbal gate, or speech, the sign is that of having become mute. Normally a person cannot stop chattering, wanting to talk about this and that in the form of gossip—all kinds of verbal engagement that are simply devoted to filling up the time, or for entertainment, or are designed to hurt someone. Here, all of that ceases. The sign for that is to be literally dumbfounded; the practitioner begins to experience things as if they were mute. This experience of muteness is powered with the knowledge of secrets. The verbal aspect in relation to the signs is activated through the empowerment of the secret initiation.

As for the third gate, which is the mind, the sign here resembles a bird. If thoughts or emotions that have arisen in the mind can be caught as soon as they arise, then there is no room for deviation, just like a bird caught in a cage.

Furthermore, a general sign of the integration of the body, speech, and particularly the mind—is to have deepening devotion and respect for the past masters, seeing them as living buddhas. The practitioner will have developed spontaneous compassion, not the compassion that develops through causes or reasons—and will truly understand how the karmic cause and effect relationship operates. They will have the ability to deal with gross levels of emotion when and as they arise, and will also be imbued with the understanding of the non-divisibility of bliss, clarity, and non-conceptuality.

Again, this understanding will occur naturally; it is not sought or developed with effort. When this manifests, the meditator will not experience normal distractions. When Mahamudra teachings speak about the three levels of the yoga of one-pointedness, this stage corresponds to that. Such a person would be established in the practice and in touch with their own true condition and would never, ever be placed in a situation where they would be compelled to break the samaya vow, the spiritual pledge. That being the case, from then on, such a meditator can never enter into lower states of existence.

The Vision of Increased Experience

When the practitioner continues with the practice as described in the text, there is no doubt that they will start to have various experiences indicating progress on the spiritual path. These fall into two categories which are: the experience based on one's understanding (Tib. *shes nyams*), and the experience connected with visions (Tib. *snang nyams*).

In regard to shes nyams, the experience connected with understanding, as the meditator pursues the practice, they will encounter episodes of bliss, clarity, and non-conceptuality, but these are sullied and therefore corruptible. Even when temporary mental clarity is present from time to time, such an experience is not completely reliable. When this happens, it is subject to fluctuation, so at times, the meditator may have a lot of confidence in their experience and practice and at other times, that is lost. For this reason, the meditator cannot rely on such experiences as an ultimate guide.

The experiences connected with visions are more reliable since the visions arise in the first place because the practitioner has had some contact with their own true condition. These visions are manifestations of the innate wakefulness which has been activated. When the meditator is more familiar with this primordial sense of wakefulness, that gives rise to various visions where one may perceive light formations endowed with the five colors.

The practitioner can and often does have a variety of experiences related to visions. These are always tied up with the perception of lights—vertical lights, horizontal lights, checkered lights, lights in the form of a dome, lights shaped like the stalk of a lotus, wheels shaped like a *vajra*, or precious stones, and various implements.

There are also various symbolic representations, archetypal symbols associated with auspiciousness. There is no limit to the shape or form that a particular vision can assume—it is completely indefinite.

All these light forms have to do with activation of the potentiality inherent in the five wisdoms. When lights are perceived in vertical form, that is the manifestation of mirror-like wisdom. When perceived in horizontal form, it is the manifestation of wisdom of equanimity. When perceived in rectangular form, that indicates the wisdom of discrimination. The wisdom of all-accomplishment manifests in the form of checkered light, and the wisdom of all-encompassing space, or the wisdom of ultimate reality, is connected to the vision of a dome.

The sign of mirror-like wisdom is that one may have the experience of sparkling sensations. Due to the activation of the wisdom of equanimity, visions of a checker-like pattern arise, similar to a net. The wisdom of discrimination is connected to the perception of flowers and so on. The wisdom of all-accomplishment connects to the perception of implements and various objects, and wisdom of all-encompassing space, or the wisdom of ultimate reality, may give rise to a perception of a dome or mandala.

The visions the practitioner may have through their practice are considered to be more important than the fluctuating experiences of bliss, non-conceptuality, and mental clarity. All these visions are connected with the development of the potentiality of the five wisdoms.

These visions of ultimate reality go through gradual transformation. At first they are small but then they gradually increase in size. The size of the object presented to the vision may initially be the size of one cubit,[43] and it then gains in magnitude. The visions of circles, thigles, do the same thing. At first the circles are very tiny in appearance and gradually they grow to the size of basins and expand to the point where a whole valley is filled with the circle of light, and the area of one's place is pervaded by the circle of light. So this is in relation to the visions of ultimate reality and it indicates the practitioner's proficiency at meditation.

Other signs associated with meditative progress include unusual behavior associated with the body, speech, and mind.

In relation to the body, the practitioner may not view it with conventional modesty. It is as though the person is stricken with an illness that compels them to act in unusual ways. This may happen from time to time.

In respect to speech, the person speaks as if they are overcome by madness. This is because the practitioner is not subject to ordinary standards of discourse, which are instigated by delusion.

Mentally, one would also experience occasional periods of cessation of mental activity, almost like a person who, having consumed poison, is rendered unconscious. This means that ordinary mental activities have come to cease, those activities that are vitiated and embellished by anger, resentment, jealousy, and so on—and whatever arises in the mind becomes settled into the natural state of the mind. It does not mean one has in fact become unconscious. It means whatever arises in the mind does not waver from the dual characteristics of the natural state of the mind, emptiness and luminosity, the characteristics of kadag, primordial purity, which is the same as the natural state of the mind.

These are some of the signs and indications of potential progress normally experienced with the practice of meditation, and the practitioner goes through these alone.

The way in which the practitioner views the world, relates to it, and interacts with other human beings will change because they have been able to free themselves from fixation on substantiality of appearances. Equipped with this knowledge or understanding, the meditator is no longer bogged down by thoughts of friends and enemies, thoughts that are closely tied up with the very strong emotions of excessive attachment or hatred. These intense passions are responsible for one's character, built on the basis of the psychic imprints left behind by such emotions. The meditator has a greater capacity to let go and not hang on to the way they are affected by others.

The meditator may also not want to be constantly occupied with the pursuit of pleasure and avoidance of pain and would not have strong dualistic reactions to happiness and pain, good and bad, acceptance and rejection. Their mind is no longer so rigid in the way that it habitually responds to different stimuli, and there is a sense of freedom from fixation. These experiences are the fruition or end result of the empowerment of non-conceptual wisdom, the fourth empowerment in the tantric system.

At this point, the practitioner has a real understanding of non-substantiality, and in the Dzogchen teachings, this stage of development is referred to as "the flight of a bird." The image of bees hovering around flowers extracting pollen is also used to convey this stage. Various commentators have compared this stage of Dzogchen on the level of thogal, to the Mahamudra stage of the yoga of non-conceptuality. It seems more appropriate, however to equate this particular level of thogal to the yoga of one-flavoredness in the Mahamudra system. If a practitioner has been able to secure this position, then they have found true liberation and therefore this particular stage of development is also referred to as "separation of samsara from nirvana." The practitioner is no longer at the mercy of karmic traces and dispositions and is not forced into assuming undesirable and grotesque forms of existence, because such a person has the ability to take on whatever appropriate form of embodiment they wish. At the time of death, the meditator will be able to make use of *osel*, the experience of luminosity, in the bardo state. Such an individual will find total liberation either here or hereafter.

The Vision of Awareness Reaching Fullness

As stated previously, there are two types of visions. The visions of space or ying, become all-pervasive in the sense that wherever there is space, there is a vision of ying. As for the visions of circles or thigles, these visions also go through changes where the circles become larger and larger. They can appear as large as a shield or the outer perimeter of a drum. They can appear singly, or manifest in numbers of five, or nine—there is complete flexibility in terms of how they manifest. Within the circles themselves, it is possible to perceive images such as a four-petaled lotus and to see visions of peaceful beings encased in the circles. These beings may appear naked, without clothes, ornaments, or jewellery.

The visions of beings are initially perceived as single. They may also appear in a combination of five, and in consort with a partner. They may also multiply to the point where they are everything that can be perceived. It is also possible to have the experience of a vision in relation to one's own body, where each pore of the body can be seen as a buddha-field, and within each pore of the body is not only the vision of one buddha-field, but of thousands.

When having these visions, for a time one's sensory impressions of material things, such as earth, rocks, mountains, rocky cliffs, and so on, may cease. Even if these ordinary sensory perceptions are not interrupted, however tiny the object of one's visual perception may be, such as an atom, a strand of hair, a leaf attached to a branch of a tree, within each of these one can have visions of buddha-fields.

Envisioning buddha-fields does not necessarily mean one is looking into some kind of paradise. It means that the full richness of ultimate reality can be seen in everything that is perceived, and every little thing can become something of significance. These visions are an expression of that particular psychic breakthrough.

To call the various perceptions of these visions "buddha-fields," is only a way of describing that experience.

In brief, visions attained on this level cannot easily be described, because words are not adequate to fully convey the kind of visionary experiences a meditator may expect to encounter at this level. All the potential experiences of the bardo have already been actualized. Due to the practice, one has already come into contact with the types of visionary experiences that a practitioner may potentially have in the bardo state.

For example, when the practitioner is undergoing these experiences, it is possible to think that there is a rope of light emanating from the heart, which then becomes embedded in the visions of varieties of beings. Above one's head, the practitioner may feel that there is a multi-colored wheel of light, just like peacock feathers. There are many different wheels of this nature. Just as in the bardo experiences, one may have visions of sambhogakaya manifestations with the wrathful deities appearing above one's head, the peaceful deities appearing in front of oneself, and below, the manifestations of nirmanakaya.[44]

The Signs of Spiritual Progress

Corresponding to these visions are the indications, the signs of spiritual progress.

In relation to the body, this indication is described as an elephant emerging from mud. Through this experience, physical objects do not provide resistance to such a person, precisely because one has realized the natural purity of the inner and external world, and understood the non-substantial nature of the internal and external worlds.

The speech is comparable to the speech of a mythical Tibetan creature. According to the myth, this creature has an amazing voice and whoever hears the sound falls in love with it. In a similar way, whatever is said by the practitioner who achieves this level becomes dharmic and is made authentic, even though literally only one thing may have been said. However, when the utterance is heard by people with different predilections and personalities, each of them will interpret it according to their needs, and thereby receive benefit from it. In one instant, such an individual has the capacity to relate to different people at many different levels.

As for the mind, it can be compared to someone who has recovered from the plague. Someone who has experienced plague and survived has no fear or anxiety about having a relapse. Anyone able to sever the ties between samsara and nirvana has no feeling of uncertainty regarding regression, no fear of being plunged back into the samsaric condition. A person of this calibre has developed all their potentiality and thereby possesses all the common and unique characteristics of enlightenment.

Here it is said that the person may be able to fly, to soar into space, or to be submerged in the depths of the earth. It is impossible for such a person to be disturbed by disharmony in the elements. This kind of person has the capacity to perform certain miracles as a result of having attained power over their own limiting conditions. People who have attained this level have been able to do so because they have fully understood and actualized the essence of the word, or logos empowerment. At this point, the meditator has fully understood the triple aspects of buddha's being, the dharmakaya, sambhogakaya, and nirmanakaya. The fruition stage, buddhahood, has been attained in this very lifetime.

In the literature, this stage is generally compared to the small and medium levels of the yoga of non-meditation in the Mahamudra teachings, but what has really been attained here is no different from the yoga of non-meditation of the highest level. There are three sources of mental delusion responsible for the perpetuation of the samsaric state, and these three are connected to the misrepresentation or misperception of the body, the phenomenal world, and the mind. Those delusory thoughts have now ceased. Of the two types of mental obscuration, those of emotional conflict and conceptual confusion, the obscuration of conceptual confusion has now been removed.

The practitioner has been able to perfect the force of knowledge or insight, compassionate and loving concern, and power, and since these three capacities have been perfected, there is no further development to be spoken of. There is nothing that one needs to develop to improve oneself.

The Vision of the Exhaustion of Dharmata

Following on from the previous vision is that known as "the exhaustion of dharmata," or "the exhaustion of ultimate reality," which is the final vision. It is given this title because the outer phenomena, or the empirical world as perceived by the senses, has merged with the inner space, ying, the space of the authentic condition. There is a sense in which a process of devolution is taking place, as opposed to evolution, where the physical aspect of buddha's being, which is the nirmanakaya, merges into the dharmakaya, the authentic state of buddha's being.

In such a state, the individual is no longer distracted by various projects requiring utilization of the body. Resulting from that is the inner experience of complete composure. The mind is not disturbed by thoughts such as regret, ambition, or aspirations—they are all exhausted. The mind has been emptied of all these processes.

In brief, what is taking place is that lhun grub, which was spoken about in great detail at the beginning of the text, and is the spontaneous manifestation of the various experiences that arise in the mind, has merged into the state of kadag, the original state of absolute purity. That is why this vision is known as "the vision related to the emptying of ultimate reality."

The spiritual signs associated with this particular attainment are as follows:

In relation to the body, one feels like a bird that was caged for a long time and has now been freed. This means that the individual does not need to utilize the body with a sense of purpose in mind.

In relation to speech, such a person uses speech like an echo. This image is used because whatever that individual says, echoes in the minds of the listeners, and is understood and interpreted in a way most relevant and appropriate to each person. However in this context, a person who has attained this state does not indulge in thoughts of the speaker and those who are spoken to.

In relation to the mind, one feels like a person who has suffered a heart attack. If someone has a heart attack and is not immediately attended to, they are going to die. When the process of death sets in, that person would have experiences in relation to the body, the functioning of the senses, and the operation of mental activities, where the bodily sensations stop, the senses become less active, everything becomes blurry, and the mind is unable to think and conceptualize clearly. In that sense, the person experiences the emptying of all activity.

In a similar way, just as a person who is dying of a heart attack cannot choose, and has to go through the dying process and face death, the practitioner in this state has no choice and is almost powerless—they are virtually pushed into attaining enlightenment. This has occurred because all the normal functions of the mind have merged into the authentic state of the individual and the ultimate reality.

When such a person has attained the goal of enlightenment, it is impossible to enumerate how the various signs, qualities, or attributes of the realized being may manifest, in terms of the spiritual signs commonly available to others.

The text, *Dra Thalgyur*, says:

> Once the meditator directly perceives ultimate reality,
> then the experience is such that it cannot be

conceptualized. One cannot entertain thoughts about it, or even express in words what has been experienced. Once this experience is well-established, giving rise to many experiences and visions, then the deluded perception starts to diminish.

The vision of deluded perception decreases as the pure perception increases. As the experiences and visions of the ultimate reality increase, then conversely there is a diminution, a decrease of the illusory perception. At this point, the meditator has actualized the real power and capacity of rigpa, self-existing awareness. Due to this vision, the meditator has fully realized the potentiality of the three aspects of buddha's being.

Because of this, the path has already been actualized. The path is no longer a path to travel on, but has become the goal. The vision of the path has taken place so there is transcendence. The path itself is realized as the goal and therefore, transcendence has been achieved. The meditator is then able to empty the ultimate reality of all its content, namely delusion, illusion, and distorted perception, to put an end to the continuous experience of the triple world.

In this way, the meditator goes through the four visions: the vision of manifest dharmata, the vision of increased experience, the vision of awareness reaching fullness, and the vision of exhaustion of dharmata.

The Three Principles of Non-wavering

The four visions are able to provide the meditator with a real sense of experience. However, just thinking about these four visions is not enough, because one must persevere with the practice and work on the four visions. This is achieved by observing what are known as "the three principles of non-wavering." The practitioner must base their practice on these principles, and by doing so the four visions will be fostered, enhanced, and developed.

The three principles of non-wavering are related to the outer, inner, and secret aspects of oneself.

The first principle has to do with one's perception of the external world. Whatever one sees or perceives through the senses reveals itself to be the buddha-field, because this principle involves maintaining pure perception.

The next principle of non-wavering is related to one's body. The meditator sees their body as an illusory body. Being present with the illusory body frees the individual from illusory experiences that lead to distraction.

The third principle of non-wavering is the secret aspect, which has to do with the movement of psychophysical energy or prana. When the practitioner remains present with the prana and is not wavering, then they have realized the marriage of the authentic state of one's being which is space, and wisdom: ying and yeshe. These two elements, which constitute the authentic state of one's being, cannot be brought together, and because of that they cannot be separated—they function in the state of totality of one's authentic condition where both elements are present.

Three Signs in Relation to Rigpa

When rigpa has fully developed, three signs will occur in relation to that experience.

The first sign is recognizing the mind and prana, the psychophysical energy, and at this point, the meditator achieves real mastery over the flow of energies. The meditator can, and often does, go through the perception of infinity and is able to establish the proper gaze, the manner in which the eye organs are used.

At this level, the practitioner has many other experiences associated with travelling on the paths and the stages of enlightenment. Someone who has secured this position has complete control over their destiny, including their rebirth. This is because a person of this stature has the body of light. However, this does not mean that the individual has ceased to exist, because the individual is still an embodied being. The individual existence of the person concerned persists almost as a reflection. The body is no longer the body of old, but has been transformed.

This form of embodiment is compared to the reflection of the moon in water. With this kind of embodiment, the practitioner will continue to benefit all beings, and there is no time limit placed on that. As long as the samsaric world has not been emptied of deluded sentient beings, the meditator who has attained this state will continue to work for them.

The second attainment associated with this level of realization is called "power over the entrance," meaning "power over the entrance into one's own true condition." Although the meditator is in possession of this very special body, the body of light, due to a lack of auspicious coincidence, they may be forced to enter into a permanent state of quietude, as beings receptive to the messages this special individual has to deliver may not be available. In such a case, that practitioner may not only decide to go into a permanent state of quietude but they may take others with them. It is said that up to three thousand other individuals may be liberated, whereupon no physical bodies remain.

The meditator's individual state of being has merged into the authentic state of being, where the physical embodiment and wisdom remain in a state of total unity. There is no separation or coming together of the physical embodiment and wisdom, which means a state of total unity. This state, once attained, is continuous.

Indications in Dreams

There are other experiences associated with this level of realization. Even when one is asleep, the dreams one has will be more significant. When the meditator begins to recognize the nature of the dreams, this in turn will be reflected in one's physical actions and how one communicates verbally with others. In traditional teachings, this type of experience is referred to as "a tortoise placed in a bowl." This means that when dreaming, those individuals capable of exerting themselves through intelligence can become completely liberated, and delusion and illusion can be brought to an end.

The meditator maintains a continuous state of luminosity day and night, whether doing various chores during the waking hours, or while sleeping. An individual who achieves this level of realization may not be as successful as someone with the type of attainment described previously, but even so, an individual with some real understanding of rigpa will find liberation or enlightenment at the time of death in the bardo, the intermediate stage.

It is possible to have a kind of premonition of one's future bardo experience during one's current dreams, where they do not lead to confusion and provide further material for delusory thoughts. The meditator is able to recognize the dreams as being dreams and as not real. Other individuals who are not as bright, nor as hard-working, are not in the same league as those described earlier, but in this very existence they will have no nightmares and only pleasant dreams and, in about 500 years, such individuals would achieve final enlightenment.

This kind of thing is talked about not only in relation to the Dzogchen teachings but there are sutras that allude to these kinds of experiences as well. For example, *The Sutra of the Light of Gold*, and a well-known Mahayana sutra, *The Ten Bhumis* or *The Ten Levels of the Bodhisattva*, elaborate on the dreams that a practitioner may experience at advanced levels of realization. The visionary dreams described in these sutric teachings correspond to the descriptions of visionary dreams in the Dzogchen or maha ati system.

The practitioner may have dreams of climbing a mountain of gold, travelling to the stars and sitting on the sun and moon. They may also dream of various forms of light emanating from their body, and then that radiating out in all directions, whereby others' suffering is alleviated. If the practitioner has prophetic dreams of this kind, then this is a sign of superior spiritual achievement.

The Four Types of Confidence

In conjunction with the four visions, the practitioner will go through the experience of the four types of confidence, which are either upward-directed or downward-directed. The ultimate reality is dual-faced: it has the aspect that is upward-directed in terms of transcendence, but it also has the downward-directed aspect that is embedded in one's condition as an ordinary person and exists within one's confusion, mental obscuration, and defilements. Other ways of expressing it would be "the transcendent experience of confidence" and "the experience of confidence in the state of immanency."

The first type of confidence is that the practitioner is able to overcome all forms of fear and anxiety, fear not only associated with physical manifestations but fear directly related to one's psychological state.

The second type is that the individual does not have fear regarding the hell realm. The hellish experiences of heat and cold, and the suffering generated, are completely transcended. In brief, the practitioner is no longer in the grip of anxiety or depression. So that kind of confidence is established within oneself at that point.

The third is when the practitioner realizes that they will no longer have to take rebirth and remain in cyclic existence or samsara, and so they have real confidence in terms of becoming enlightened and possessing and developing the qualities of an enlightened being. These manifestations of confidence in relation to fearlessness are connected to the confidence of the empirical kind, or directed to one's condition as it is.

The fourth kind of confidence, which is confidence developed by the practitioner in relation to the realm of the transcendental, comes about through not feeling desperate to attain nirvana or to experience the fruition of nirvana.

So three types of confidence are directed toward the present realm, the realm of temporality, and the fourth one is directed toward the transcendental realm. These four types of confidence are attained through having full understanding that the samsaric experience and the nirvanic experience, the realm of temporality and the realm of the transcendental, are both expressions of self-existing awareness, an experience which is direct and non-mediated, non-conceptualized.

Fundamentally, it all boils down to the understanding that there is nothing with enduring essence and that one cannot fully articulate the true existential condition of the ultimate reality.

When the Dzogchen practitioner has had these experiences then, without deliberately following the system of paths and stages as laid out in the sutric and tantric teachings, these levels are accomplished automatically.

The Paths and Bhumis

According to the sutric teachings, the orthodox or exoteric teachings of Buddhism, five paths are involved in relation to one's journey to enlightenment: the path of accumulation, the path of application, the path of seeing, the path of cultivation, and the path of no more learning. These five paths correspond to ten stations or levels of spiritual development, known as *bhumis* in Sanskrit.

According to the esoteric teachings, sixteen stations are involved with one's spiritual progress. The tantra, *Luminous Sphere*, says that according to the tantric and Dzogchen approach, the path of spirituality is traversed instantaneously. There are also five paths in relation to this approach. For example, when the student engages in the practice of ngondro, the preliminary practices, and starts to perform Guru Yoga, this corresponds to the path of accumulation. As the student goes further and receives instructions from the teacher on the practices of trekcho and thogal, that corresponds to the path of application as presented in the sutric teachings.

Eventually, the introduction of the mind takes place between the student and the teacher. This is accomplished through four different methods of pointing-out instructions. The first is example, the second is meaning, the third is sign, and the fourth is symbol. From this, the practitioner is able to establish full confidence in attaining enlightenment in this very life. This corresponds to the path of seeing.

Finally, there is the meditation of non-meditation, the meditation practice devoid of a goal, which corresponds to trekcho practice, and then the practice of nothing to meditate upon, which is the thogal practice of leaping over. These practices, in turn, are referred to as being the path of cultivation stage. These two approaches to Dzogchen practice are unified and there is a real sense of balance. That balance is not achieved by joining together two separate entities that could still be separated since they were different beforehand. They are primordially non-separable and because of that, there is balance. This corresponds to the path of no more learning, because at that point the meditator has understood and mastered the real human condition.

The practitioner of Dzogchen comes to understand that samsaric bondage, the freedom of nirvana, and the path that leads to nirvana—all of these experiences have their origin in the mind. Without mind we could not speak about anything, there would be no bondage, there would be no freedom, and there would be no path to speak of.

According to Dzogchen teachings, it is said that the individual must traverse the path and proceed along the ten stations of spiritual development, however if an individual is able to understand the existential condition, how things exist, then the stations of spiritual development are realized instantaneously. At this point, someone who has followed the exoteric tradition of Buddhism may wonder, "How is that possible?" If the pointing-out instructions regarding trekcho and thogal are appropriated properly, then one would experience the result of the ten stations of spiritual development, as laid out in the exoteric traditions.

When the individual has connected with the pointing-out instructions in terms of trekcho and thogal, an enormous sense of relief and joy arises in their mindstream. That corresponds to the first station or level of spiritual development known as "the joyous station."

As the practitioner continues with the practice, the inner experiences that arise due to the workings of the mind or sensory perceptions are seen as being dependent upon the mind. The mind is the creator of everything experienceable. This corresponds to the station of stainless, the second level.

As the meditator becomes more acquainted with and skilled in the practice, they are able to apprehend the real nature of things, and that corresponds to the third bhumi or spiritual station known as "luminosity" or "luminous."

The meditator then begins to realize that the real nature of things and phenomenal appearance are not separate. With that realization, one attains the fourth spiritual station known as "brilliance," which has to do with the deepening of one's meditative experiences.

This then leads to the meditator being able to overcome all conflicting emotions. The meditator need not try to divorce themselves from delusion and conflicting emotions—they are seen as self-purifying. This corresponds to the fifth station known as "hard to train."

At the sixth station, the meditator is able to make use of the circles of the sun, as mentioned earlier in the text. The circles assume various forms and present themselves to the meditator. This station is known as "actualization." Here, the meditator has been able to firmly grasp the significance of rigpa, self-existing awareness, according to the Dzogchen teachings.

At this point, the meditator is no longer disturbed by the goings-on of the samsaric condition, and has turned away from habitual tendencies. This particular station of spiritual development is known as "far gone," which means the practitioner has departed from all that they were familiar with in the past.

This is followed by the eighth spiritual station, where the meditator is no longer disturbed by conceptual proliferation, hence this station is known as "unwavering," the "non-wavering state."

When the meditator is completely at ease with the phenomenal world, is able to see it as a mandala in itself and complete in itself due to powers associated with wisdom, and with complete control over the domains of experience of the phenomenal world, this corresponds to the ninth station, "sublime intelligence," eventuating in wisdom itself.

Everything experienced comes under the purview of wisdom where everything, the visual field and the sensory fields, becomes completely transformed and manifests as clouds in the sky, arising from the ocean. This particular station of spiritual development or bhumi, is known as "cloud of dharma," or "cloud of the phenomenal world." In this context, "dharma" does not mean the teachings, but the phenomenal world—everything that exists, material things, and psychological states as well. That corresponds to the tenth station, "the cloud of dharma."

So far, the discussion has been about how the esoteric teachings of Dzogchen correspond to the exoteric teachings of sutra. The discussion has not allowed for where the differences lie, and these are many. As will become clear, the esoteric teachings of Dzogchen are superior. If we were to single out some of the main differences, then it would have to be said that the following is quite a fundamental one.

According to the exoteric teachings of sutra, the ten stations of spiritual development of the bodhisattva, who is the spiritual practitioner of the exoteric teachings, are secured through great effort. The bodhisattva applies the ten paramitas or transcendental actions of generosity, moral precepts, patience, vigor, concentration, wisdom, qualities, equanimity, renunciation, and activity. This involves enormous effort and hardship, yet one may still be left with dualistic thoughts. Because the practitioner may not really understand the unity of the sensory fields and the subject, there is still a possibility that they may be caught up in a dualistic mode of thinking.

In the context of Dzogchen, which is part of the esoteric teachings, the path has to be traversed in a speedy manner. Unlike the exoteric teachings where it is said that one needs to spend three countless eons to achieve ultimate fulfillment, here, according to the esoteric teachings, without a great deal of effort or exertion, if one practiced properly, one could achieve an enormous sense of fulfillment in a matter of months and years. The body as it is now could be transformed into the authentic expression of one's body, and the environment, the world, could be transformed into a buddha-field. The individual could appreciate and enjoy all of this through having understood the self-existing awareness within their own mindstream.

How is this extraordinary achievement possible? According to the esoteric teachings, this is possible because instead of thinking of karmic cause and effect and conflicting emotions as something to be abandoned, discarded, and be rid of, they are seen as self-purifying. The conflicting emotions, karmic tendencies, and conceptual proliferation are seen as self-freeing and self-purifying. Because of this, the esoteric teachings are exceedingly superior.

The Tantric Teachings

Having discussed the teachings of the exoteric tradition, we can now discuss the esoteric teachings in terms of the inner tantric teachings.

In Tantricism, pleasure is emphasized, and the practitioner, through applying various yogic methods, is able to induce four states of bliss. This is achieved by transforming conflicting emotions in their own home ground. The Dzogchen teachings however go further and do not rely on the esoteric methods, let alone the exoteric methods mentioned before.

How so? It is precisely because a practitioner of Dzogchen realizes the necessity for the cultivation of osel, translated as "self-existing awareness"—and the various manifestations of that awareness. Dzogchen practice is orientated toward apprehending the reality as it is, in an immediate way. Immediacy is emphasized in the Dzogchen teachings, rather than resorting to methods such as those employed in the esoteric teachings.

The Dzogchen practitioner then has to develop full confidence and certainty in what has been perceived, because what one has perceived is very close and not at a distance. The perceiver and the perceived are not separated. The subject and object, the perceiver and the perceived, are brought together with self-existing awareness.

In terms of phenomenal presentation, whatever is perceived is seen as lights. Everything reveals itself and because of that they are seen as lights, illuminating. This direct experience of the phenomena causes certain psychic perturbations, psychic changes, in relation to the five forms of psychological disturbance—desire, anger, jealousy, pride, and ignorance. But when the phenomena are apprehended in an immediate way, they reveal themselves as being completely different—instead of psychic perturbations, one has the manifestation of five wisdoms, with the qualities of the object present in terms of color.

The meditator may have immediate experience of things that in reality are not even in existence. In terms of sensory impressions, various shapes and colors may be perceived. If one has been practicing the esoteric method of Tantricism, then many kinds of perceptual objects will appear that do not correspond to anything in the real world, such as gods and goddesses in sexual union, and one will be able to perceive a whole spectrum of the mandala.

That is one kind of experience that can come from Dzogchen practice. What is happening here is that the perceiver and the perceived are no longer seen as being different. That notion of apprehender and apprehended, perceiver and perceived is suspended. That is what emptiness means, according to the Dzogchen teachings: "original purity not vitiated by thoughts of duality."

This kind of attainment is inexplicable. It cannot be put into words or articulated in any way because it has to do with direct experience. What this amounts to is coming close to the existential reality. The ultimate reality is very close, but it is not something to be seen. It cannot be seen because it is unconditioned and what is unconditioned is not amenable to the senses. Seeing what cannot be seen by realizing that what one had thought was at a distance is actually close, is realization, actualization. What was potential is now made actual.

According to Dzogchen, the stations of spiritual development can be multiplied. In the exoteric teachings of the sutras, there are ten bhumis, and in the esoteric teachings, there are more. With the Dzogchen teachings, they multiply until there are sixteen stations of spiritual development in terms of the visionary experiences that have been described so far. These visions manifest subsequent to the various stations of the spiritual practice experienced by the practitioner.

However, the Dzogchen practitioner should realize that it is not so very important to talk about the various spiritual stations on the path, or one's journey to enlightenment. That is because according to the sutric teachings, a bodhisattva may traverse the five paths and ten stations of the exoteric approach to the practice, and once the latent, unresolved, conflicting psychic tendencies are overcome, they become enlightened—whereas, from the tantric perspective, if one has been able to achieve that, then the eleventh spiritual station has been attained, the station of Akanishtha, so this is equated with the eleventh bhumi or spiritual station.

According to the tantric teachings, the practitioner may go even further to the next level of spiritual attainment, the twelfth bhumi, which is known as "Lotus of non-attachment." Then one becomes completely enlightened and this attainment of enlightenment is equated with the thirteenth bhumi, "the vajra-like" or "indestructible state." This is where all one's potential qualities and attributes emerge. What was hidden has now become completely obvious and apparent—it is no longer latent. According to Dzogchen teachings, that is no big deal, because what is important is to have confidence in awareness. By having efficiency and dexterity in the practice of awareness, then whatever is experienced will be seen as an expression of Akanishtha, the unconditioned reality where there is no division, no divisiveness.

The practitioner realizes that whoever one is, this existing individual manifests the enlightened qualities, because the state of enlightenment is contingent on causes and conditions that are present in the individual in themselves. The Dzogchen practitioner has to understand that these causes and conditions are spontaneously present within the existing individual. Instead of thinking in terms of surpassing, or traversing the various levels of spiritual development, there is realization of oneself as that individual, with the potential to become enlightened or who is already the embodiment of enlightenment.

Tsele Natsok Rangdrol says that he will not elaborate on this too much, for fear of confusing people.

The Lesser Modes of Liberation

So far we have described the way in which a person of superior intellect achieves liberation in one lifetime—however, an individual practitioner can attain liberation through other means. For example, a person of lesser intellect has the opportunity to achieve it in the postmortem state of the bardo, and a third alternative is available whereby the individual can secure liberation by realizing one's spiritual being.

There may also be circumstances where the practitioner has become familiar with the Dzogchen teachings and is able to maintain conviction in and inclination toward these teachings, however they may not have done any serious practice in their life. A person of that nature can still expect to be liberated in the postmortem state. There is a text on the bardo written by the author of *The Circle of the Sun*, Tsele Natsok Rangdrol, called *The Mirror of Mindfulness*, so there is no need to go into detail here. The methods of achieving liberation are explained in a detailed way by other teachers as well. Those texts that discuss such alternative modes of liberation should be consulted.

In this context, we are concerned about the mode of liberation attainable in this very lifetime, as opposed to the other forms of liberation. How is that goal obtained? It is obtained by relinquishing one's hold over the samsaric condition, relinquishing one's hold on worldly, non-spiritual concerns, and instead practicing the two methods of Dzogchen, namely trekcho and thogal. If the practitioner can apply themselves to these two methods, even if they are unable to free themselves immediately due to certain spiritual obstacles, they will be able to achieve liberation in this very lifetime through the power of spiritual instruction. It is inevitable that this will happen.

Conversely, instead of focusing on the practice, if a person simply hovers around the edges of spiritual practice, becoming familiar with certain teachings and acquainted with some level of practice, they could develop an inflated sense of self and become egotistical due to such involvement. That person may merely recite familiar words and phrases on the topic of emptiness, say, and they may be very eloquent in using various forms of expression, and may talk as loudly as possible. But if the individual has not internalized the teachings and the various methods of meditation and related that to one's existential condition, then one's character has not been touched. There is not even a trace of real spirituality present in the practitioner.

If the person is unable to really practice and relate to their existential condition, they could be very familiar with concepts such as liberation and attainment, and hundreds of thousands of words and terms may constitute their vocabulary, but that person is no better than an ordinary person who has not even thought about enlightenment or liberation. They will not be going anywhere other than wandering in the samsaric condition, and will actually risk plunging further into the depths of despair of samsaric existence. I am sure that any thoughtful reader of this text would understand that, so I do not want to overindulge myself in terms of the importance of practice.

Enhancement

So far, the text has briefly described the view and meditation. In keeping with tradition, something should also be said about action, and according to Dzogchen teachings, the method is known as "effortlessness, spontaneous action." The Dzogchen practitioner should be learning how to be spontaneous, so that they do not feel constrained in any way. This is something that one has to actualize. If one is unable to do that, then one would not fully understand the depth of Dzogchen experience. The reader should keep in mind that what is said regarding action is provisional. What follows constitutes the essence of the Dzogchen approach toward behavior and ways of being. Texts such as *Coming Together of Sun and Moon* have spoken about the twenty-one different modes of physical expression available to a practitioner, but here we will concentrate on the seven that are fundamental to the spiritual aspirant.

The Seven Types of Conduct

1. The practitioner should familiarize themselves with the view, meditation, and contemplation.

2. The Dzogchen practitioner should cultivate an attitude that resembles a swallow. The approach to the practice should be like that of the swallow entering its nest without hesitation. This image is used because when the practitioner is able to determine the true meaning of the spiritual instructions, they unhesitatingly enter into the spiritual home because there is no doubt or uncertainty present in the mind. In that way, the

practitioner does not get lost or distracted.

3. The focus is on the actual practice itself. Here, the meditator approaches the practice like a wounded wild beast. The invocation of this image is used because a wounded wild animal retires to a place where there is no disturbance and prepares itself for the inevitable. In a similar fashion, the Dzogchen practitioner does not get distracted by the various goings-on of the world, and learns to enjoy solitude.

4. The Dzogchen practitioner invokes the image of a mute person, a person unable to speak, because the practitioner should not overindulge in chatter and idle talk. Much idle talk is gossip, where one may say good things about certain individuals and bad things about others. Speech should not be misused. In this way, one should be like a mute person.

5. The Dzogchen practitioner should act like a madman. This image is relevant, because just like the mad person, the practitioner is not swayed by thoughts of friends and enemies, and therefore does not develop a deep-seated sense of attachment, aversion, or even indifference.

6. The sixth approach to Dzogchen practice is to make use of the image of a pig, a sow, or a boar, because the practitioner should not concern themselves with where they are, in terms of external conditions. The pig does not discriminate. According to the Tibetan way of thinking, a pig is quite happy to lie in its own waste. It is quite happy wherever it is—it does not get bothered. In a similar way, the Dzogchen practitioner should not be overly concerned with circumstances and situations in terms of their food, clothing, and bed. There is a sense whereby the practitioner is able to accommodate various circumstances and situations.

7. The seventh image used is a lion. The lion is a symbol of absolute confidence and fearlessness. Just like a lion, the Dzogchen

practitioner does not become discouraged or despondent, because they are no longer afflicted with thoughts of hope and fear, so they have freed themselves from the bondage of hope and fear. This means that the practitioner is able to rise above causes and conditions, can exercise a sense of autonomy, maintain an element of distance from the causes and conditions in their life, and resist the power of the otherness of causes and conditions.

These seven points involved with the behavioral and attitudinal aspects of Dzogchen practice should be kept in mind through the course of one's life. Finally, the practice of Dzogchen is really about freeing oneself from all concerns and worries—that is the state one is aiming for. However, until that state is secured, one should concentrate on developing compassion and becoming a more caring and open individual. The practitioner should also have a real sense of distaste, a nauseous reaction toward the things that bring the practitioner undone. They should also be less possessive and greedy, and always apply themselves with a sense of enthusiasm.

These attitudes should be supported by the three subsidiary attitudes, being inclination toward practice, humility, and pure perception, which will foster one's spiritual practice. If this is done properly, then the practitioner would be able to bring their understanding of trekcho and thogal, the cutting through and leaping over aspects of the Dzogchen teachings, into everyday life, where trekcho and thogal become conjoined and all the practitioner's energies are centralized. It would be possible for such a practitioner to leave the samsaric condition forever but instead, they have firmly established themselves in spiritual practice.

The practitioner develops full confidence by possessing the key to the spiritual instructions. Through the realizations that ensue from the practice, everything that is experienced and experienceable, whether good or bad, spiritual or secular, reveals itself as kadag, as original perfection, which is the meaning of Dzogchen. In terms of one's experience, the origin and dissolution of all these processes occur in that very state. That is what is called "buddhahood", according to the Dzogchen teachings. To become a buddha, to become enlightened, is to attain that state.

When a Dzogchen practitioner becomes very proficient, understanding that all things experienced and experienceable are the manifestation of the original purity and original perfection, such a person will see everything. Even in terms of the sensory impressions, they themselves become spiritual teachers. Everything experienced through the senses, and even what one experiences on the samsaric level, can be self-revelatory. Such a practitioner of Dzogchen is truly blessed.

The sensory impressions have been transformed because of the practitioner's experiences in relation to the sense fields, and they are now seen as buddha-fields, meaning that everything is seen in a different light. We still see, hear, taste, touch, and smell things, but those things are done in a different way. We understand that what we smell, touch, taste, hear, and see, does not have enduring essence or substance. First, there is the emptying out process and then the filling in. Everything is back in place, yet everything is back in place in a different way. Consequently, when the practitioner encounters difficulties in life, has problems of various kinds and is placed in situations where things are not happening according to their wishes, even in those circumstances they do not become disturbed.

How so? That is because the practitioner understands that even these disturbances, if understood properly, can be self-liberated in the condition of the body of light. In this way, the practitioner is able to cut through the very root of adverse causes and conditions. Such an individual would have real understanding of the nature of the mind, where the mind is understood as being primordially pure, kadag. It does not matter what is experienced in life because all experiences arise from and dissipate back into the nature of the mind.

When the practitioner has really progressed, then they should even free themselves from thinking in terms of the practice of view, meditation, and action in relation to Dzogchen. The value associated with these is instrumental—they do not have intrinsic value as such. This will be seen very clearly by the practitioner.

The real Dzogchen practitioner has this approach to the practice. The three aspects of buddha's being find their expression through oneself, where the attainment of buddhahood takes on a different sense, precisely because buddhahood is no longer seen as an object and the practitioner as a subject—what one wants to attain is already present within oneself. This understanding of enlightenment can take place effortlessly and in a very short period of time.

That does not mean that one should forgo practice and that things will just happen—one has to practice. These are degenerate times, which are filled with conflict. Most people are actually more concerned with worldly affairs, and therefore have no interest in or inclination toward spiritual practice. Even if they do have some interest, then whatever little understanding they have only encourages them to become more egotistical. Spiritual practice is then used in order to further their own needs. Many people cannot even set aside one full day to do spiritual practice and instead, spend their time either sleeping or shopping for clothing, or stuffing their faces with food—time is wasted in that way for no reason at all. Meditators like this live in hope, but in their actual lives, nothing is happening.

It is possible that such people are acquainted with the teachings and understand what the spiritual levels are, and what the spiritual paths mean. There may also be a degree of immediate meditative experience and understanding, but even so, if they do not have the Dzogchen understanding described here, they will only live in the state of hope. The wise ones, those who are reflective, should think about this more fully.

As it is said in the *Gandavyuha Sutra*:

> If one does not translate understanding into immediate experience, then it is like a giving and generous person who wants to feed others who have no food and to quench the thirst of those dying from thirst, but who does not feed themselves, and so perishes due to lack of nutrition. Not being able to translate understanding into immediate experience through meditation is exactly the same—one is in the same situation.

and

> Without meditation one will not be able to understand one's true condition. How so? A person can see water, analyze it, know its properties and all about it, but if one has not been able to drink it, their thirst will not be quenched. Knowing water in terms of its properties and its value is like understanding key spiritual matters. Drinking the water is comparable to translating that into one's immediate experience. In this way, real spiritual practice in terms of meditation is the fundamental thing in one's life.

According to Dzogchen practice, this is the fundamental point. Buddhism in general has many kinds of practices and rituals, but even though these things are important, they are not so very important. In terms of the trekcho and thogal practice of Dzogchen, as Tsele Natsok Rangdrol has explained in his text on Mahamudra,[45] it is possible for the practitioner of trekcho to be led astray. If one has not fully understood the trekcho practice, then to engage in thogal practice would not be fitting, and would also be pointless.

If the practitioner has been able to engage in trekcho practice properly, they will not have to worry about becoming side-tracked or regressing when they become involved with thogal practice. The general tantric descriptions of the opening of the eyes through the various therapeutic methods can be read about in other texts.

Fruition

The practitioner achieves the ultimate realization, and along with wisdom, also assumes the physical manifestation of enlightenment. This is realized due to the persistence applied to the practice because according to Dzogchen teachings, the defilements, the obscurations of the mind, have to be seen as adventitious and not intrinsic. Gradually, as the practitioner progresses on the path, layers of defilements are peeled away. First the gross defilements begin to subside, then the subtle defilements dissolve by themselves, and finally even the most subtle ones will disappear. At the end, all defilements are completely exhausted.

Wisdom is nothing other than realizing that fact. As defilements decrease, wisdom increases, and that is how it is. If a person who was born blind comes into contact with a doctor skilled in restoring sight, then that person will be able to see. Beforehand, they were unable to appreciate the details of various objects. Gradually, as the blind person becomes accustomed to having sight, they will be able to observe and perceive the details of visual presentation.

This analogy is used because the blind person needs to have eye organs to begin with— without these, the blind person would not be able to have their sight restored. The physician has only assisted—nothing new is introduced, there is nothing extraneous— the potentiality for sight was already there. In a similar manner, all living beings are endowed with buddha-nature, intrinsic awareness, which is pure right from the beginning. However, that primordial purity is covered by adventitious defilements, hence ordinary sentient beings go through life as if they are blind. The innate capacity is there, but due to those defilements, the person cannot make use of it, so another kind of doctor is needed, a spiritual doctor. The physical and mental potentialities, the innate tendencies, can be brought to the fore so that one is able to make use of the eye of wisdom.

When the practitioner sees the nature of things as they exist, it is normally referred to as "the attainment of enlightenment," but this is simply a way of defining things using words. In reality, apart from definitions, the individual embodies the tripartite aspects of buddha's being and his wisdom. The tripartite aspects of buddha's being and the wisdom that has become manifest at that point are not newly acquired—nothing new has come into being.

As the delusions and defilements begin to dissipate, the practitioner's true condition starts asserting itself and becomes manifest. When the Dzogchen practitioner achieves this state of total liberation, then the psychophysical constituents as we know them are left behind. The realm of the absolute is entered into, and vanishing into the absolute can be achieved in this very lifetime. Both Mahamudra and Dzogchen agree upon this point—there is consensus.

The *Heap of Jewels* tantra says:

> When one does not conceptualize but is able to let this very mind be, allowing the sensory representations to take place, then the sensory experiences themselves become self-liberated. All experiences can then become undiluted and pure and will embody the qualities of emptiness and luminosity, because intrinsic awareness is present. Even perceptions in relation to one's body will change and the body will no longer be perceived as a product of the

elements—earth, fire, air, water, and space, because the individual has realized the unconditioned state. All delusory and illusory thoughts will become extinct. Even though experiences, thoughts, and emotions continue, the nature of those thoughts and emotions will be understood as being without origin, because they are embedded in the ultimate reality. Because of this, the meditator no longer thinks in terms of the perceiver and the perceived, because what is perceived becomes naturally liberated, precisely because the mind has become so present and aware. All embodied beings must understand this fact.

According to the thogal teachings of Dzogchen, the sensory representations will become self-liberated and therefore one's misconceptions regarding sensory objects will cease. There is realization that within one's innermost being there is wisdom, that one's innermost being is not separable from wisdom. When one is in touch with that, all the buddha-fields will be simultaneously realized. Arriving at this point, the thogal practitioner will have complete power over their destiny, even in terms of taking birth and entering into the world, because the body that has been assumed is no longer seen in the conventional manner. Instead, one sees the body as a reflection of the moon in a pond.

With this understanding, the practitioner, as an embodied person, can continue to benefit an infinite number of sentient beings. If that is not achieved during this life, then it may happen in the postmortem state in the bardo. For example, relics of their body may be left behind, and their enlightened qualities may manifest in the form of words, sound, earthquakes, rainbows, and showers of flowers. Their enlightened qualities would manifest in many different ways.

If that is not possible for the Dzogchen practitioner, then at the very least, they will be able to manifest as nirmanakaya and be born from the heart of a lotus flower, where they will receive secret empowerments and prophecies. Such an individual will be able to traverse the remainder of the path to enlightenment by eliminating adventitious defilements and karmic traces and dispositions. They will have realized the insubstantiality of thoughts and concepts, because there is understanding that one is in the true state when there is the unified experience of bliss and emptiness. This experience has become part of the practitioner. To realize that is known as "dharmakaya."

Emptiness, which is ultimate reality, and wisdom are seen as inseparable. Ultimate reality, which is emptiness, and wisdom cannot come together or be separated, precisely because they have always existed in unison, from the beginning. This authentic state of being where ultimate reality and wisdom are inseparable is known as "dharmakaya." Many people have given form to it—they visualize the dharmakaya with a face, hands, legs, and so on, and can often become so attached to the forms of dharmakaya as visualized in their daily practice that they forget what dharmakaya is really about.

Without understanding their true condition, people engage in unnecessary forms of debate and argumentation. As I understand it, and according to the Dzogchen teachings, it is possible for such people to spend endless hours debating these things, whether these images are real or not, whether they exist or do not exist—but they do not understand the real dharmakaya and how it exists in its own true condition. The dharmakaya, in terms of one's true condition, cannot be formulated in words—it cannot even be conceptualized. This is because concepts have to be thought about in relation to whether something exists or does not exist, but in terms of one's authentic existence, this does not apply.

One could spend a hundred eons pondering and conceptualizing about the dharmakaya but one would not understand what dharmakaya is, what one's true condition is. It can be realized when the practitioner is not searching, not seeking. When the practitioner allows oneself to be in one's true condition, which is incorruptible—one realizes that there is no need to be preoccupied with words, descriptions, and definitions, because one's true condition is self-manifest. This is how I understand the way that one's true condition is realized, according to the Dzogchen teachings.

The Kayas

In this manner, dharmakaya, which is the authentic state of one's being, is free from differentiation, attributes, qualities, and is self-manifesting. From that state, the practitioner projects the qualities and attributes of sambhogakaya, the symbolic aspect of one's being or buddha's being. These qualities and attributes begin to assume the forms of the five wisdoms, and the five wisdoms manifest as expressions of the mandala.

The sambhogakaya visionary experiences continue to operate effortlessly as unceasing expressions of enlightened activity. In this way, the physical expression and the mental aspect of an enlightened being become completely integrated, so that the individual is then empowered to operate in the world without obstruction and in an unceasing manner.

The third aspect of an enlightened being is the nirmanakaya. The nirmanakaya expression relies on physical gestures, interaction with other beings that takes place on the physical level, where compassion finds its true expression. The enlightened being, having embodied the previously mentioned qualities of dharmakaya and sambhogakaya, is now able to operate in the world in such a way through the physical embodiment that the needs of others are fulfilled. The way in which compassion is shown corresponds to the needs of those who the enlightened being encounters, and the number of beings that such a person is able to benefit will be countless.

It might be asked, how is this possible? How would an enlightened being, someone who had been practicing Dzogchen and has now become realized, interact with other beings when the emphasis in practice is on transcendence, detachment, and in particular not making any effort—not even thinking of enlightenment itself? Dzogchen has always emphasized that one is complete and full, as one finds oneself within one's being.

If that is so, then the whole idea of enlightened beings interacting with and benefiting others may be perceived as being quite contrary to what has been said, but this is not so. In fact, a fully enlightened being would not have thoughts of doing or doer, in terms of "myself" and "others" who are affected, or see things as discrete entities. Thoughts of myself and other, doing and doer, the act and the actor—these are not important. Due to compassion, which is a transcendental act in the sense of transcending the realm of egoism, one has truly found oneself, which is as precious as a wish-fulfilling gem, or a mythical tree able to grant everyone's wishes by producing whichever fruit they wish for. Once the enlightened being has fully embodied the necessary qualities, the richness of one's being has been discovered. Without making an effort or a deliberate choice to benefit others, that occurs naturally. This is what is known as "activity," the qualitative activity of an enlightened being.

In concluding this text, we have to say that realization of the three aspects of buddha's being is the aim of Dzogchen practice. Often in the teachings, four aspects of buddha's being are mentioned. Many classifications are used to describe the final experience of enlightenment but in brief, they can be reduced to two: *arupakaya*, the immaterial or mental aspect of buddha's being, and *rupakaya*, the material or physical aspect of buddha's being. In their true condition, the arupa and rupa aspects, the mental and physical aspects of buddha's being, do not exist separately—they exist in unison. To understand this, many examples have been used in Dzogchen teachings, such as mirrors, portraits, and rainbows in the sky.

What does this mean? This means that the relative and absolute realities cannot be separated—that is, the authentic physical expression of the body cannot be separated from wisdom. Things, entities, and empirical objects, or dharmas, cannot be separated from the true reality, dharmata. Emptiness and luminosity of the mind, reality, and phenomena, the sphere of authentic existence and wisdom, are all technical terms used in the context of Dzogchen teachings, and the practitioner has to understand the sense of unity of these terms so that they do not fall onto one side as opposed to the other. This is truly realized or actualized within one's being when one becomes enlightened, with full expression of the enlightened qualities coming through the physical aspect as well as the mind.

This is a summary of the fruition stage of Dzogchen practice from what I have been able to put together by sampling the different sources as they exist in the traditional body of teachings.

Summary

by Traleg Kyabgon

Having finished the text, *The Circle of the Sun*, I thought I would recapitulate and provide a summary.

As I went through the text, I found it so inspiring and profound—it is the best summary of Dzogchen teachings I have ever seen. It is already a very condensed text, and to summarize it will condense it even further. I recommend that it be studied and reviewed again and again. This is really very important.

The text started with the discussion of the ground, the nature of the mind. What is the starting point on the spiritual journey? There are many different kinds of starting points when embarking on a spiritual journey—there are religious conversions of all kinds. For example, suddenly, an atheist might decide to believe in God and redemption.

It may be that the starting point of the spiritual journey is in relation to who one is, how one views oneself, where one may see oneself as inadequate. At that time, the person is full of confusion, anger, jealousy, and hate, so in this case, the conversion does not take place because of some other being. It does not come from inspiration outside the person. Instead, the person begins to think that if they applied themselves in the context of spiritual practice, then they could be transformed and become someone else, be a changed person.

According to the Dzogchen teachings, all these ways of

approaching one's present condition, even before embarking on the spiritual path, are inadequate. It should be understood that what one wants to attain and realize is already there. To transform oneself spiritually, one should not be looking for external inspiration, or have this idea of a complete transformation. To seek complete transformation means that there is a gap between what one is and what one wants to become. Dzogchen and Mahamudra teachings say that there is no gap. What one wants to become is in fact what the person already is, so the only problem is not understanding where one is, what one is.

This is what is meant by "the ground," the starting point, because one's own true condition is complete. That is also what the Tibetan word, Dzogchen means: "Self-perfection," or "Great Perfection." We are already perfect in that sense. That is because one's state of perfection has the three aspects of essence, nature, and responsiveness.

Essence refers to our natural state. We cannot even speak about when in relation to our natural state. To use the word when, we are thinking in terms of temporality, whereas the natural state is beyond time. It is unconditional—it is an unconditioned state of total openness. That is the essence aspect of the true nature of being.

That unconditioned state of total openness is not vacuity, because in that state, there is a sense of luminosity, and that is the nature.

From luminosity arises the aspect of responsiveness. When the word "responsiveness" is used, that includes all our thoughts, emotions, ideas, expectations, hopes, and fears. Anything that we can think of, including our sensory responses to the world, how we interact with the world, physically, verbally, and mentally, is included in the third aspect of our ground of being. That is the starting point, the ground of being.

On the level of emptiness, which is the level of essence, the completely non-differentiated state, it is not possible to speak about causes and conditions because it is devoid of all that. Yet because of that, a sense of luminosity arises, and from that sense of cognitive presence, all other mental activities ensue. From the perspective of essence, there is no difference between tables and human beings, but there is a difference in relation to the aspect of nature, of luminosity, in terms of cognitive functions and abilities. Because of that, all the other mental functions manifest as well. That is the ground, the three aspects of the ground.

Then there is the path, and according to Dzogchen, the path rests on the practices of trekcho, cutting through, and thogal, leaping over. Trekcho practice is related to shamatha practice, settling the mind. This is not in the sutric sense of settling the mind with the use of antidotes, but instead it involves settling the mind in its own natural state without contrivance, without effort, and not thinking of thoughts and emotions as something to be rejected.

It is very similar to Mahamudra practice, but there is a difference nonetheless, which the author of this text alluded to: "According to Mahamudra, we pay attention to our thoughts and emotions and think of them as being useful." Dzogchen—not always, but by and large, emphasizes rigpa or self-existing awareness. There is no fundamental difference, because in relation to trekcho practice, thoughts are not judged. Any form of judgment, "This thought is good, that is bad; this emotion is good, that emotion is bad" is suspended. This is performed in both traditions, so in that sense, there is no real difference.

That is what trekcho practice is all about, learning to settle the mind effortlessly. The Dzogchen practice also continually reminds students not to get too attached, even to mindfulness practice. They should try not to be too mindful, but be natural, relaxed, and open, and shamatha experience comes from that. As Tsele Natsok Rangdrol says in his section on trekcho: There are many different methods used within Buddhism. We practice shamatha meditation, tantric practices of visualization, breathing practices, yogic exercises, and so on. That is not really as important ultimately, from the Dzogchen perspective, because what is important is to learn to settle the mind.

In relation to trekcho practice, Tsele Natsok Rangdrol mentioned the Four Yogas of Mahamudra and compared that to the four experiences of Dzogchen.

The first yoga is the yoga of one-pointedness. According to Mahamudra, the practice of one-pointedness is viewed in relation to three stages—that indicates there is development taking place. There is an initial stage of one-pointedness, the medium stage of one-pointedness, and then the final developed stage of one-pointedness. Here, the meditator is concerned with stabilizing the mind, stilling the mind. At the beginning of one-pointedness, the experience is compared to a waterfall, because thoughts come and go, there is agitation present, mental disturbance, and so on.

In Dzogchen, the experience of one-pointedness is not divided into three stages, but instead "the experience of stability" is spoken of. According to the author, as far as the practice goes, there is no difference—nonetheless, they do not speak about the initial, middle, and developed stages of one-pointedness.

The second yoga is the yoga of non-conceptuality or yoga of simplicity. Here, the practitioner has made considerable advancement for the simple reason that they are now able to perceive that they have the nature of ultimate reality. On this level, conceptual proliferation has subsided and emotional disturbances have also found their resting place.

Dzogchen and Mahamudra teachings have sometimes had differences at this level, because certain Mahamudra masters have felt that Dzogchen teachings encourage practitioners to slip into the quietude of shamatha or mental tranquility. Dzogchenpas do not see a problem in this context, because of their emphasis on rigpa, or awareness. Dzogchen does not have initial, middle, or advanced stages of simplicity. Instead, they refer to this as "the experience of unmoving samadhi."

The third yoga is the yoga of one-taste, which means that the meditator realizes that there is no distinction between samsara and nirvana, confusion and wisdom. There is a real sense in which the meditator realizes a sense of unity in everything. What they experience is full of diversity, but the nature of what is experienced is not differentiated or determinate. Whether it is physical, mental, subject, or object, everything is seen as having the same experience. For that reason, in Dzogchen it is referred to as "the experience of equality." The author says that sometimes the Mahamudra teachings may make use of the concepts of meditation, post-meditation, and so on, but strictly speaking, these do not apply.

The fourth yoga, the yoga of non-meditation, is the same as attaining buddhahood. A total state of non-duality has been realized, where even the thought of meditation has been left behind because the meditation object, the meditator, and the practice of meditation have become one. In Dzogchen this is called "the experience of spontaneous presence." In that way, the practitioner of trekcho also goes through various levels of stabilizing the mind with vipashyana meditation.

Then we come to thogal practice, leaping over. Thogal practice basically involves making use of various images and visions, and through them, realizing one's innate wakefulness. Whatever one experiences externally is seen as the reflection of one's innate nature, so there is no difference between the visions one is experiencing and who one is as a practitioner. The idea of overcoming duality is expressed there.

I will briefly summarize the four lamps. The first lamp is the penetrating water lamp, or the far-reaching water lamp, and refers to the eye organs, the eye consciousness, and the wisdom consciousness working in unison. To practice thogal, the eyes must be open and one should be looking at the sky, a physical lamp, or even if the windows are slightly open in a dark room and a stream of light is coming through, one should look at that, but one does not look at the light directly. The penetrating water lamp is the starting point. While practicing that, many different shapes and forms can be seen that are not physically present, but are caused by the sunlight or whatever source of light there may be. This is considered to be very important in thogal practice.

The second lamp is the lamp of pure space. When these shapes first appear, they are erratic, always moving, and because of this, one's head and the eye organs might move when trying to focus on them. The shapes are vague and indistinct, but over time become more stable and distinct because one begins to see these visions in the context of space. The visible manifestation of these images is no longer just in the foreground, but one begins to see them as having a background, a horizon.

Many techniques are used to activate this kind of practice. The Tibetan text mentions going to the ocean, seeing where the ocean and the sky meet, and sitting there at sunset or sunrise. One doesn't literally look at the sun—that may not be such a good idea—but when doing the practice, it is possible to see many different visions. I am actually not teaching thogal practice. I am only speaking about thogal practice, so I will not say too much about this. Using the hands as a screen, it is possible to look at the sun whereby the sun can be streaming down and all kinds of visions can be seen there.

The third lamp is the empty bindu lamp. As one progresses, one begins to see bindus, circles of light. Initially, the circles may be a single color, but gradually, one begins to see multi-colored, five-colored visions of circles. At first, there are only a few, and then they multiply and become more and more colorful. The more colorful they become, the more greatly valued they are according to Dzogchen teachings. If they assume the colors of a rainbow, they represent one's innate potentiality for wakefulness in relation to the five wisdoms—the five colors of the circles represent one's own five innate wisdoms.

The fourth and final lamp is called "the lamp of self-existing knowledge," and is regarded as the most important one. The lamp of self-existing knowledge is no different from self-awareness or rigpa. In Dzogchen, there is a significant difference between sems and rigpa. Sems is our ordinary empirical consciousness that thinks, anticipates, remembers, plans, gets worried, becomes anxious, and so on. Rigpa is not like that. Rigpa, or self-existing awareness, is aware of everything that is going on. All of the lamps lead to realization of "the lamp of self-existing knowledge."

There are also four visions involved in thogal practice. The first vision is the vision of manifest dharmata. We are becoming familiar with the lamps—they are the foundation, and then the real visions start to take place. Here, one will have visions of many different things, from the very smallest to the greatest. It is possible to have visions of houses among multiple things. The practitioner does not try to manufacture or give rise to these visions—they are not created. That point needs to be emphasized. One simply sits there and lets the images come.

The second vision is that of increased experience. The practitioner can have many different experiences related to visions, and can see varieties of patterns and flowers—there is no limit to what can be perceived. Increasingly, the practitioner knows that all these visions are manifestations of oneself.

The third vision is the vision of awareness reaching fullness. Here the visions change and one begins to perceive not only circles but the forms of deities—many gods and goddesses either in union or alone. In brief, one begins to see real forms of beings.

The fourth is the vision of the exhaustion of dharmata, dharmata meaning "reality." At this point, the visions have vanished—the deities, mandalas, circles—everything spoken about so far has vanished. They are no longer perceived by the practitioner, precisely because one has attained one's true condition, and all the visions have been taken on board and integrated.

That leads to the last section of the text, which is the fruition stage. At the fruition level, the practitioner realizes the three aspects of an enlightened being.

The first aspect is dharmakaya, the unconditioned aspect of one's being, which is the same as the essence of one's own nature, as described at the beginning of the commentary.

The second aspect relates to the visions that have been spoken about, which are manifestations of the sambhogakaya aspect of one's being, the symbolic expressions that come from one's innate nature.

Lastly, one's physical being, which is utilized in all these practices, is the nirmanakaya or physical expression of buddha's being, because even the physical aspect has been transformed through the practices of trekcho and thogal. The body is used because the visions rely on the workings of the body, the breath, and the mind. How these visions are experienced is also contingent on one's physical condition—how one's nadis, the psychophysical channels, are functioning; how one's chakras, the psychophysical energy centers, are operating; how one's life-essence or bindu is working; and how these operate together. At the fruition level, the practitioner begins to realize all three aspects of buddha's being in this way.

Notes

Introduction

1. Yana: commonly translated as vehicle, yana is a Sankrit/Pali term for any means of transportation. In the Mahayana tradition, the term is used to refer to a mode of transportation on the path to enlightenment. More specifically, the term yana, or vehicle, is used to refer to different sets of teachings that enable one to journey to enlightenment.

2. Nyingma: literally "old school," it is the oldest of the four major schools of Tibetan Buddhism. It is also often referred to as *Ngangyur*, "order of the ancient translations." The Nyingma school is founded on the first lineages and translations of Buddhist scriptures from Sanskrit into Tibetan in the eighth century, during the reign of King Trisong Detsen (r. 710–755).

   Nyingma traditional histories consider their teachings to trace back to the first Buddha Samantabhadra (*Guntu Sangpo*) and Indian mahasiddhas such as Garab Dorje, Sri Simha, and Jnanasutra. Traditional sources trace the origin of the Nyingma order in Tibet to figures associated with the initial introduction of Buddhism in the 8th century, such as Padmasambhava, Yeshe Tsogyal, Vimalamitra, Vairotsana, Buddhaguhya, and Shantaraksita. The Nyingma tradition is also seen having been founded at Samye, the first monastery in Tibet. Nyingma teachings are also known for having been passed down through networks of lay practitioners or *ngagpas*.

   Nyingma teachings include a distinctive classification of Buddhist vehicles to liberation, called the nine vehicles. This schema places the Nyingma teachings of the "Great Perfection," or Dzogchen, as the highest of all Buddhist teachings. As such, the Nyingmas consider the Dzogchen teachings to be the most direct, profound, and subtle path to buddhahood. The most influential Nyingma scholar yogi of the Great Perfection is Longchenpa (1308–1364), and his voluminous works mark a turning point in the scholastic systematization and refinement of the Nyingma Dzogchen system.

The Nyingma school also has an important tradition of discovering and revealing "hidden treasure texts," called Termas, which allows the treasure discoverers, or *tertons*, to reveal new timely scriptures. Many Nyingma lineages are based on particular termas.

3. Luminosity: unlike inanimate objects, the mind is luminous. Mind is able to illuminate both itself and other things. The luminosity of mind is not something that is discovered outside our ordinary experience. Sometimes people call luminosity "clear light," but that is only a symbolic expression. It refers to a tremendous sense of clarity where you see things precisely, instead of having a foggy mind, and as opposed to dullness and depression. From that point of view, it is luminous.

4. Raton Ngawang Tenzin Dorje: (18th-19th century) was a disciple of the omniscient Jikme Lingpa who wrote a commentary on *Yumka Dechen Gyalmo*, known as the *Ra Tik*, in 1801.

5. Gotsangpa Gonpo Dorje: (1189-1258) was a mahasiddha of the Drukpa Kagyu school, well known for his songs of realization and said to have been an emanation of Milarepa. He was born in southern Tibet, but moved to Central Tibet, where he met his main teachers Tsangpa Gyare Yeshe Dorje and Sangye On. Following his studies, he travelled from one isolated hermitage to another, never staying in the same place twice. He founded the branch of the Drukpa Kagyu school

known as the Upper Drukpa.

6. The Drukpa Kagyu: a branch of the Kagyu school of Tibetan Buddhism. The Drukpa lineage was founded in the Tsang region of Tibet by Tsangpa Gyare (1161–1211), a student of Ling Repa, who mastered the Vajrayana practices of the Mahamudra and Six Yogas of Naropa at an early age. As a terton, or "finder of spiritual relics," he discovered the text of the Six Equal Tastes, previously hidden by Rechung Dorje Drakpa, the student of Milarepa. While on a pilgrimage, Tsangpa Gyare and his disciples witnessed a set of nine dragons (Tibetan: *druk*) roaring out of the earth and into the skies, as flowers rained down everywhere. From this incident they named their sect Drukpa.

    Within the Drukpa lineage there are further sub-schools, most notably the eastern Kham tradition and middle Drukpa school which prospered in Ladakh and surrounding areas. In Bhutan the Drukpa lineage is the dominant school and state religion.

7. Milarepa: (1028/40–1111/23) a Tibetan siddha, who was famously known as a murderer when he was a young man, before turning to Buddhism and becoming a highly accomplished Buddhist disciple. He is generally considered one of Tibet's most famous yogis and spiritual poets, whose teachings are known among several schools of Tibetan Buddhism. He was a student of Marpa Lotsawa, and a major figure in the history of the Kagyu school of Tibetan Buddhism.

8. Tsuglag Gyatso, the Third Pawo Rinpoche: (1567–1630) an important lineage of Karma Kagyu masters very closely associated with the Karmapas. The Pawo tulkus were at the head of Nenang Monastery in U-Tsang, Central Tibet.

9. Jatson Nyingpo: (1585–1656) a Nyingma master and terton or treasure revealer. His main terma cycle is the *Konchok Chidu.*

10. Kagyu Lineage: translates to "Oral Lineage" or "Whispered Transmission" school, one of the four main schools of Tibetan Buddhism. The Kagyu lineages trace themselves back to the 11th century Indian Mahasiddhas Tilopa, Naropa, Maitripa, and the yogini Niguma, via their student Marpa Lotsawa (1012–1097), who brought their teachings to Tibet. The Tibetan Kagyu tradition gave rise to a large number of independent sub-schools and lineages. The principal Kagyu lineages existing today as independent schools are those which stem from Milarepa's disciple, Gampopa (1079–1153), a monk who merged the Kagyu lineage with the Kadam tradition. The Kagyu schools which survive as independent institutions are mainly the Karma Kagyu, Drikung Kagyu, Drukpa Kagyu, and the Taklung Kagyu. The Karma Kagyu school is the largest of the sub-schools, and is headed by the Karmapa. Other lineages of Kagyu teachings, such as the Shangpa Kagyu, are preserved in other schools. The main teachings of the Kagyus include Mahamudra and the Six Dharmas of Naropa.

11. Jamyang Khyentse Chokyi Lodro: (c. 1893–1959) a Tibetan lama, master of many lineages, and a teacher of many of the major figures in 20th-century Tibetan Buddhism. Though he died in 1959 in Sikkim, and is not so well known in the West, he was a major proponent of the Rime movement within Tibetan Buddhism, and had a profound influence on many of the Tibetan lamas teaching today.

12. Dilgo Khyentse Rinpoche: Tashi Paljor, Dilgo Khyentse Rinpoche was a Vajrayana master, scholar, poet, teacher, and recognized by Buddhists as one of the greatest realized masters. Head of the Nyingma school of Tibetan Buddhism from 1988 to 1991, he is also considered an eminent proponent of the Rime tradition.

13. Tsele Natsok Rangdrol's biography ref: rigpawiki.org

14. Ngondro: the preliminary or "foundation" practices of Vajrayana Buddhism. The ngondro practices are profound and powerful means for effecting a deep purification and transformation, at every level of our being. Not only do they prepare the practitioner for the profound path of Vajrayana, and teachings of Dzogchen, but they also lead him or her gradually toward the experience of enlightenment.

15. Samsaric: Samsara is commonly translated as "cyclic existence," "cycle of existence," et cetera. It can be defined as the continual repetitive cycle of birth and death that arises from ordinary beings' grasping and fixating on a self and experiences.

    Specifically, samsara refers to the process of cycling through one rebirth after another within the six realms of existence, where each realm can be understood as either a physical realm or a psychological state characterized by a particular type of suffering. Samsara arises out of *avidya* (ignorance) and is characterized by *dukkha* (suffering, anxiety, dissatisfaction). In the Buddhist view, liberation from samsara is possible by following the Buddhist path.

16. Mahamudra: The highest meditation training of the Sarma or New schools of Tibetan Buddhism, and a special feature of the Kagyu lineage.

Prologue

17. The Dzogchen teachings were divided into three divisions, or cycles, by Manjushrimitra, one of the early masters of the Dzogchen lineage, a disciple of Garab Dorje and the main teacher of Shri Singha. These three divisions are the Mind Cycle (Tib. *semde*), the Space Cycle (Tib. *longde*), and the Cycle of Secret or Pith Instructions (Tib. *mennagde*). Shri

Singha further divided the mennagde into four cycles of outer, inner, secret, and innermost unexcelled. The core of the mennnagde are the teachings of *nyingtik*, or "Heart Essence" teachings, that were revealed to Jigmey Lingpa in three visions of Longchenpa in the late 18th century. The four divisions, or cycles referred to by the author are the four divisions of the mennagde.

Section One

18. Eternalism: The belief that there is a permanent and causeless creator of everything. In particular, that one's identity or consciousness has a concrete essence which is independent, everlasting, and singular.

19. Nihilism: Literally, "the view of discontinuance." The extreme view of nothingness. No rebirth or karmic effects, and the non-existence of a mind after death.

20. Samantabhadra: In the Dzogchen teachings, our true nature is represented by Samantabhadra (Tib. *Kuntuzangpo*), depicted as a buddha, deep blue in colour, sitting naked in the vast expanse of space, and encircled by an aura of rainbow light. He is completely naked, meaning unstained by any trace of concept, and represents the absolute, naked, sky-like primordial purity of the nature of our mind.

21. Vajrasattva: the sambhogakaya buddha Vajrasattva is the sovereign of all the buddha families and mandalas. The lineage of Dzogchen is traced from the dharmakaya Samantabhadra to the sambhogakaya—the five buddha families and Vajrasattva, who are Samantabhadra's own self-reflection.

22. New Schools: Sarma or "New Schools" refers to the schools of Tibetan Buddhism that follow the later translations of Buddhist texts from India, made from the time of the great

translator Rinchen Zangpo (958–1055) onwards. The schools in this category are Kagyu, Sakya, Kadam, and Gelug.

23. Mahayana Buddhism: (Tib. *tek pa chen po*) Literally, the "great vehicle." These are the teachings of the second turning of the wheel of dharma, which emphasize shunyata or emptiness, compassion, and universal buddha-nature. The purpose of enlightenment is to liberate all sentient beings from suffering as well as oneself. Mahayana schools of philosophy appeared several hundred years after the Buddha's death, although the tradition is traced to a teaching he is said to have given at Rajgriha, or Vulture Peak Mountain.

Section Two

24. Kamadhatu, rupadhatu, and rupadhatu: The three realms of existence of sensuality, form, and formlessness

25. Lamrim: A Tibetan Buddhist textual form for presenting the stages in the complete path to enlightenment as taught by Buddha. In Tibetan Buddhist history there have been many different versions of lamrim, presented by different teachers of the Nyingma, Kagyu, and Gelug schools. However, all versions of the lamrim are elaborations of Atisha's 11th-century root text *A Lamp for the Path to Enlightenment*.

26. The five wisdoms: The transformation or transmutation of the negative emotions, known as the "five poisons," into much more enhancing forms of psychic, life-enhancing energy. The five poisons of desire, aggression, jealousy, pride, and ignorance are transformed, or transmuted, into their corresponding five wisdoms. Desire is transformed into discriminating wisdom, aggression into mirror-like wisdom, jealousy into all accomplishing wisdom, pride into wisdom of equanimity, and ignorance into wisdom of dharmadhatu, or reality.

27. Maha Ati: The Sanskrit term for Dzogchen

28. Shravaka: Meaning "one who hears and proclaims." There are two explanations. The first is that the shravakas first hear the instructions from the Buddha on teachings such as the four noble truths or the twelve links of interdependent origination, and then through reflecting and meditating on these instructions they attain their fruition of arhathood.

    The second is that the shravakas receive or hear teachings on the Mahayana from the Buddha, and although they do not practice them themselves, they retain them with their infallible memories.

29. Pratyekabuddha: Meaning "solitary realizer." People who have embarked on a spiritual path independently of any tradition and without a teacher. They attain the level of a pratyekabuddha arhat by themselves, in solitude.

30. Twelve Interdependent links (Tib. *nidanas*): (1) ignorance, (2) karmic formations, (3) consciousness, (4) mind-body complex, (5) six sense fields, (6) contact, (7) sensory impressions, (8) craving, (9) clinging, (10) becoming, (11) rebirth, (12) decay, old age, and death.

    These twelve links are like an uninterrupted vicious circle, a wheel that spins all sentient beings around and around through the realms of samsara.

31. Bodhisattva: A practitioner of the Mahayana who, having given rise to bodhicitta, has vowed to attain enlightenment in order to free all sentient beings from samsara. The term encompasses ordinary beings but is particularly associated with those who have attained the enlightenment of the bodhisattva levels.

32. Shravakayana: Literally, "the lesser vehicle." The first of the

three yanas or vehicles. The term refers to the first teachings of the Buddha, which emphasised the careful examination of mind and its confusion. It is the foundation of Buddha's teachings, focusing mainly on the four truths and the twelve interdependent links. The fruit is liberation for oneself.

33. Meditative gaze: Generally, in Hinayana and Mahayana meditation, the gaze is lowered and relaxed, whereas in the Tantric method, the eyes are wide open, challenging. This is evidenced in portraits of siddhas such as Padmasambhava, Tilopa, et cetera.

34. Garab Dorje: (55 CE) Garab Dorje received all the tantras, statements and instructions of Dzogchen directly from Vajrasattva and Vajrapani, and became the first human vidyadhara in the Dzogchen lineage. Having reached the state of complete enlightenment through the effortless Great Perfection, Garab Dorje transmitted the teachings to his retinue of exceptional beings. Manjushrimitra is regarded as his chief disciple. Padmasambhava is also known to have received the transmission of the Dzogchen tantras directly from Garab Dorje's wisdom form.

35. Yongdzin Lodro Gyaltsen: (1552–1624) A master famous for his writings in defence of the Nyingma school and his history of the Vajrakilaya teachings.

36. Savaripa: (10th century) One of the eighty-four mahasiddhas of India. Shavaripa was a hunter who turned to the Buddhist path and renounced his livelihood after an encounter with the bodhisattva Avalokiteshvara. He later became a disciple of Nagarjuna, and a teacher of Maitripa. Shavaripa is a key figure in the transmission of the early Mahamudra lineage of teachings in India, and counted among the "Indian Patriarchs" of the Kagyu lineage.

37. Panchen Sakya Shri: (1127–1225) A major Kashmiri sutra and yogini tantra commentator. The Tengyur lists 23 works attributed to Sakya Shri as an author.

38. Chisam Namkha Drak: (1210–85) An important Kadampa master associated with Narthang Monastery. He was the teacher of Chomden Rigpe Raldri, Pakpa Lodro Gyaltsen, and others.

39. Kaduk Yagdey Panchen: a search for information on Kaduk Yagdey Panchen was ineffective.

40. Nub Ben Yonten Gyatso: Born in 1260 in a family that practiced the Nyingma tradition in the Dok region of Tsang. He first studied at Dar Monastery, where he became an expert in Abhidharma and epistemology.

41. Tibetan renaissance of Buddhism (950-1150): At the time of the introduction of Buddhism to Tibet in the 8th and 9th centuries, the early Buddhist philosophers were the Nyingmapa's, known as "the Old School." Buddhism was almost completely wiped out during the rule of King Langdarma (803–846). In this context we are speaking about the cittarva, which means the period "after Langdarma." Buddhism was re-established in Tibet with the development of the Kagyu, Gelugpa, Sakya, and Kadam traditions, known as the sarmas, "the New Schools." This revival was driven by the translators, lotsawas, who searched for authentic Indian Buddhist texts to be translated into the Tibetan language, and also studied and practiced under great Indian Buddhist masters.

42. Five skandhas: Five aggregates that describe the collection of phenomena that is taken to be a self, and are associated with grasping onto the self—form, feeling, perception, formation,

consciousness.

43. Cubit: An ancient Indian measurement, a cubit is the length from the elbow to the tip of the longest finger.

44. The wrathful visions of the deities allow the transformation of what in psychological jargon might be called the dark side of the psyche. The wrathful deities represent our hatred, resentment, traumas, fears, anxieties, all of those things. This happens even when dreaming. When we dream and have a nightmare, we see beings, and often they are beings that may not normally exist, but are a product of our own imagination brought about by whatever unresolved psychic tension is there. It means that we do not only come in touch with the positive aspects of ourself as symbolized by peaceful beings, or deities or whatever we want to call them, but we also are able to transform and change those aspects of ourselves that we find difficult to come to terms with.

45. Tsele Natsok Randrol's book on Mahamudra, *Notes on Mahamudra* was translated as *The Lamp of Mahamudra* by Rangjung Yeshe Publications and Shambhala Publications.

Index